CANOEING AND KAYAKING WISCONSIN : THE RIVERS, THE TOWNS, THE TAVERNS

BY DOC FLETCHER

Canoeing and Kayaking Wisconsin: The Rivers, The Towns, The Taverns
© Doc Fletcher, 2011

ISBN: 1-933926-28-7
ISBN 978-1-933926-28-5

Arbutus Press
Traverse City, Michigan
editor@arbutuspress.com
www.Arbutuspress.com

First Edition/ First Printing

Printed and bound in the United States of America

Maps © Maggie Meeker, 2011
Illustrations © Keith Jones, 2011, Bigtimeartguy, Inc.
Photos © Doc Fletcher, 2011

CONTENTS

ACKNOWLEDGMENTS

Thanks to my wife and best friend Maggie who brings joy to my author's journey through her love, enthusiasm, ideas, support, companionship, and participation.

Thanks to my parents and family for their abundant love and support.

Thanks to my friends, spiritual brothers and sisters, for the love that they give so freely.

Thanks to the crack research team members for being wonderful river companions and for their inquiring minds.

Thanks to the Bigtimeartguy and my 4Day brother, Jonesey, for sharing his gift and contributing his fabulous illustrations to my books.

Thanks to those canoers and kayakers who leave the rivers cleaner than when they started.

Thanks to Andy's Seney Bar for the Dickel and for finding my river shoes.

Thanks to the folks at Olympus for helping to make the photos reflect the beauty of the rivers and surroundings.

Thanks to the local historical societies, chambers of commerce, livery owners, librarians, those met at taverns, and fellow paddlers along the way, all who shared their stories.

Thanks to all of those who come out for my library talks, for bringing your enthusiasm and for making it fun.

Thanks to the radio and newspaper interviewers for taking the time to get the word out.

Thanks to Arbutus Press and Susan Bays for your publishing expertise and direction.

Thanks to Mike Svob for your exceptional paddling books.

Thanks to the Mobil Lounge Softball Team & Beer Swillers Club for a quarter-century of Thursday night magic. You load Sixteen Tons and what'd ya get?

Thanks to God for all the blessings that I've been given.

PREFACE

A day on the river is a week of happiness. This book has been written as a guide to get you into the middle of that happiness as easily as possible. I've always believed that to get the most enjoyment out of a day on the river, there are three ingredients that should be a part of that day:

1)   the river,
2)   the town,
3)   the tavern

Each of these three ingredients is included when you read about a river trip in this book. Twenty-one rivers are detailed in the book and each gets their own chapter. That chapter begins by providing the reader with information about a river trip including:
    • The river's "degree of difficulty" so that you know if this river is appropriate for your paddling skills. There are three degrees of difficulty: beginner – a good river for your first time out, intermediate – you should know how to steer a canoe, veteran – this challenging requires past paddling experience,
    • A suggested trip down the river, usually a two to four hour adventure,
    • The suggested trip length in miles and time,
    • A map of the suggested river trip,
    • Noting key landmarks on the route that act as your "clock on the river" so that you can gauge where you are on the water versus the trip's total time; some landmarks are more permanent in nature (e.g., merging creeks, riverside homes, bridges) and some are less so (e.g. : logjams, beaver dams), but all are included to provide as many time points along the way as possible,
    • Providing full details about a canoe & kayak livery that can both rent boats or offer hauling and car spotting if you bring your own boat,
    • And letting you know how many miles it is to the livery town from various towns in Wisconsin.
    After a river trip is outlined, the chapter shares the history of a town near the river. The "town" section always begins by telling you where to turn the dial to find the local radio station affiliate for the Milwaukee Brewers and the Green Bay Packers, so that you can keep track of the teams while paddling away from home. The reader learns interesting history about the town, making the river experience that much more enjoyable.
    Each chapter concludes by directing you to an old time tavern in that town, a place that serves a great bar burger and a Pabst Blue Ribbon, or a Schlitz, or a Leinie to go with it, making your great day on the river that much more memorable.
    A "bonus" river has been added to the book, the fascinating architectural and historical paddle down the Chicago River. This was added not because we are geographically challenged necessarily, but rather this 21st chapter was inserted among the 20 Badger State rivers as a not so "hidden trek", a great trip to take on your way north to paddle Wisconsin.
    Rivers are only included if they are serviced by a canoe & kayak livery, so that the joy of a trip down that river is accessible to

everyone, whether they own their own boat or not. Livery owners are passionate about their rivers, they want to share that passion with their customers, and they always put safety first. It seems that, no matter how many times you paddle a river, you always learn something new about that river when you talk to livery owners. Examples of how livery owners enhance your trip's safety and enjoyment are by matching your paddling abilities with certain river stretches, pointing out portages or other obstacles, telling you to avoid the river if it's running too fast today to have a safe float, and advising you to come again another day when the water level is higher so that you're not just walking the river.

Canoe & kayak liveries perform an important service for all paddlers, whether you use their services or not, one that is often overlooked: they are the ones who remove the fallen trees and the deadwood from the water to keep the rivers free flowing for all of us.

To assist you in planning for your paddling adventures, this book includes a "Paddling & Camping Checklist" and a list of canoe & kayak liveries for rivers throughout Wisconsin.

Each river trip was documented using (1) a digital voice recorder to make note of the key landmarks and obstacles along the way, (2) a GPS to track the miles and the hours & minutes from the trip beginning to when each landmark would be reached as well as total trip miles and time, and (3) a waterproof digital camera to record the beauty that is the Wisconsin rivers.

Each chapter notes the month that the trip was taken. In general, this is helpful as the water levels will be higher in the spring, from spring rains and winter snow pack melt down, and lower in the summer months. Higher water levels bring speed to a river, and trips taking five hours in the summer can take three hours in the spring. In *general*, the water flows faster in the spring and slower in the summer, so noting in each chapter when the trip was taken can be a useful river speed gauge. The key phrase here is *in general*.

Mother Nature sometimes upsets how water flow follows the changing calendar. An example of this occurred on the Lemonweir River. The Lemonweir trip for this book was taken in May, when the river was a slow and meandering float. Normally the river would be moving even slower later in the summer as river levels drop. But unusually heavy rains two months after the May trip turned the laidback Lemonweir into a rampaging river that, in the case of the *Country Cruisin' Kayaks & Canoes* livery, flooded their land, knocked over one of their buildings, swept away a canoe trailer and various canoes and kayaks, and made the river too fast to safely paddle.

If you're traveling from Michigan to these Wisconsin rivers, consider traveling across Lake Michigan on one of two car ferries, either the Lake Express (from Muskegon to Milwaukee, 866-914-1010) or the *S.S. Badger* (from Ludington to Manitowoc, 231-845-5555). Both are great experiences.

Each chapter includes a musical soundtrack, because music brings as much beauty and happiness to us as rivers do. Mostly though the soundtracks are included just for fun. The soundtrack tunes are songs that are in some way connected to the experience on the river, or in the town, or in the tavern, or in the state of Wisconsin, or simply because of the love of the song. Each chapter soundtrack kicks off with a song by a Wisconsin-based band (except the Chicago River soundtrack songs which are all by musicians with ties to the Chicago area) including many classic instrumentals from the 50s and 60s - think The Ventures and Hawaii Five-O. Check out "Elemental Instrumentals" on the Ace label for your next drive to a river.

Every time we get into a canoe or a kayak, it's a chance to reach out and touch history. Despite all of the technological advances that come at us in waves on a daily basis, the boats that we float today down rivers are little different in basic design than the boats used hundreds of years ago by the original residents of Wisconsin to traverse down the rivers. The river is the cure for the common day. Enjoy every moment on it that you can.

Regards,
Doc Fletcher

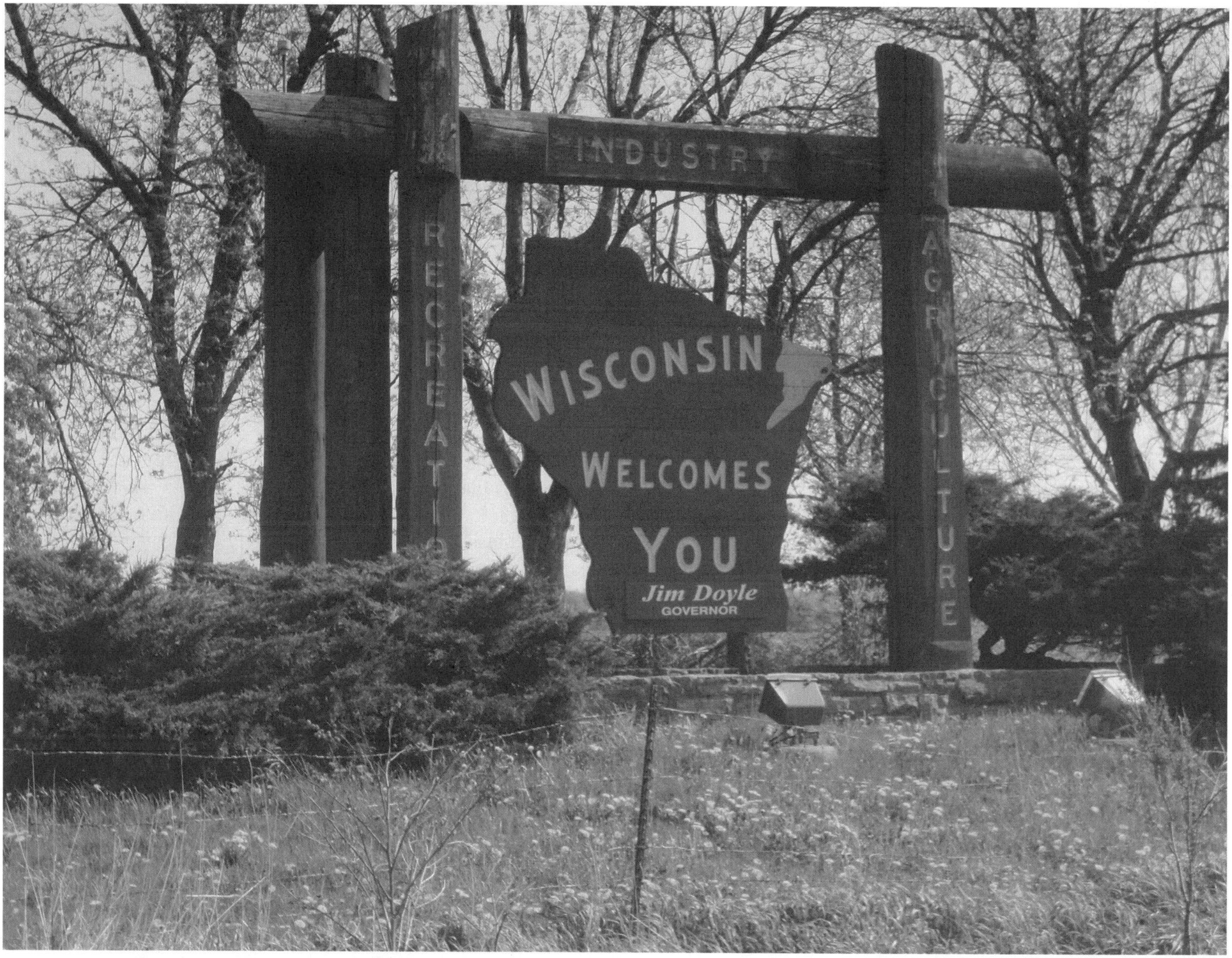
INDUSTRY
WISCONSIN
WELCOMES
YOU
Jim Doyle
GOVERNOR

DEDICATION

TO THE MEMORY OF OUR SWEET LITTLE **ROSIE**

BARABOO RIVER

THROUGH BARABOO WISCONSIN

TRIP 7.7 MILES/ 2 HOURS 30 MINUTES

Veteran Ability Required

LIVERY: RIVERSIDE RENTALS
103 ASH STREET, BARABOO, WI 53913,
(608) 356-6045 OR (608) 434-2468.
OWNER JON HILLMER

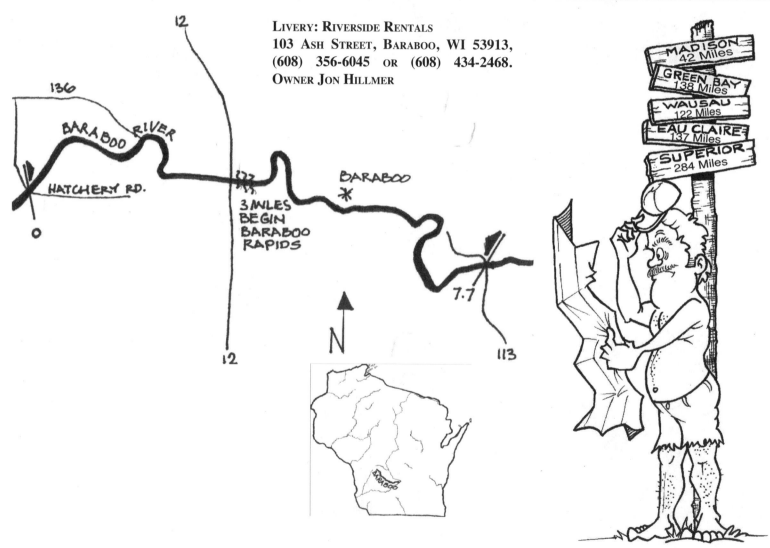

MADISON 42 Miles

GREEN BAY 138 Miles

WAUSAU 122 Miles

EAU CLAIRE 137 Miles

SUPERIOR 284 Miles

12

136

BARABOO RIVER

HATCHERY RD.

0

3 MILES BEGIN BARABOO RAPIDS

BARABOO *

7.7

12

113

N

THE BACKGROUND: BARABOO RIVER

SOUNDTRACK: SLIPPIN' AND SLIDIN' – THE CITATIONS, SUMMER WIND – TONY LoCRICCHIO, GHOST RIDERS IN THE SKY – VAUGHN MONROE, RINGLING RINGLING – JIMMY BUFFETT, STANDING BY A RIVER – CLIMAX BLUES BAND

RIVER QUOTE: JON: "THE BARABOO IS THE USA'S LONGEST UNDAMMED RIVER EAST OF THE MISSISSIPPI." MAGGIE'S REPLY: I'M SURE PEOPLE WHO TIPPED OVER HAVE DAMNED IT."

The Baraboo is a river that once experienced you'll want to get back on again as quickly as possible. It flows SE 120 miles from its headwaters near the town of Kendall until it empties into the Wisconsin River south of Portage, but it's through the town of Baraboo that the river really picks up the pace: here the gradient gets steep as the river drops 10' per mile (45' over 4 ½ miles), providing canoeists and kayakers with a terrific class 1 and 2 paddling experience.

There's excellent fishing on the Baraboo with runs of Croppies, Rainbow Trout, Smallmouth Bass, and a chance to haul in 3' long Sturgeon.

Paddling the stretch of the Baraboo outlined in this chapter offers a bonus not found on any other river, anywhere: you are floating through the original grounds of the Ringling Brothers Barnum & Bailey Circus. It is a river memory that you'll never forget.

Baraboo paddlers were Bret Holbrook, Kenny Umphrey, and Doc. The trip was in May.

THE RIVER: PADDLING THE BARABOO

Launch west of town from the Hatchery Road Bridge, paddle through downtown Baraboo, and take out at the Highway 113 Bridge boat ramp.

Putting in a few yards upstream from the Hatchery Road Bridge, the river is 50' across and 8' deep. Upon launching, you're at the start of a one-half mile long straightaway. During the first hour of the trip, the current is very slow, nothing like what awaits you downstream in Baraboo.

.8 mi/18 min: a creek merges from your left, 12' wide at its mouth.

.9 mi/21 min: along the right bank is open land with "caution gas pipeline" signs.

1.2 mi/26 min: a winding 30' wide creek merges at a severe angle from the right, just before the river takes you beneath power lines.

1.6 mi/37 min: Highway 136 sits on a high bluff along the left bank. We're getting continuous sighting of geese and ducks along this stretch of the river.

2 mi/43 min: you'll know that you're exactly 2 miles into the trip when you see a pretty little spring on your left that drops 2' to the river at the base of a willow tree. Another 1/10th of a mile downstream, also on your left, a big crevice cuts its way through the land on its way to the Baraboo River.

2.2 mi/48 min: arrive at the 1st of 2 old railroad spur abutments (the rail line is now gone) which today is now a midstream grassy island with a large rock base. Over the next few minutes, the flat contour of the land on the left shore shows where the trains once ran.

2.3 mi/49 min: a 20' tall rock outcropping sits on the right bank.

The Baraboo Rapids begin!...

3 mi/1 hour: float beneath the Pine Street (Highway 12) Bridge & enter the Baraboo city limits. On the approach to the bridge are two rock

and driftwood islands, both serving as homes to large geese nests on our trip. Beginning just before the Pine Street Bridge, and extending beyond, are class 2 rapids. The water churns enough to come over the top of the canoes. Stay right through these rapids. Just downstream is an old mill on your left as you approach a driftwood island.

3.4 mi/1 hr 10 min: Haskins Park, with toilets and picnic facilities, is on the left. At the downstream end of the park is the Shaw Street Bridge. On the approach to the Shaw St. Bridge is the twin of what you saw at the 2.2 mile mark: a grassy island with a rock base that was an old rail spur abutment. Whitewater develops around the next bend.

4 mi/1 hr 20 min: the Baraboo River Walk on the left shore is fronted by a beautiful stone seawall. Just beyond the seawall and River Walk sits the 26 acres of the Ochsner Park & Zoo. Beyond the right bank is a power grid. You're into a great whitewater run, and it's a long one, continuing just beyond the next footbridge.

4.3 mi/1 hr 27 min: the old wool mill on the right bank is immediately before the 2nd Avenue Bridge. You paddle through class 2 rapids at the bridge.

5 mi/1 hr 40 min: you're paddling under the Broadway Bridge (Business Route 12).

5.2 mi/1 hr 43 min: you float beneath the Vine Street Bridge and are looking downstream at the wildest rapids run today, an exciting, brief and challenging class 2. The run begins immediately after the gazebo on the left shore and ends 1/10th of a mile away at the Ash/ Walnut Street Bridge. Stay left of the two islands for the safest route.

 5.3 mi/1 hr 45 min: the rapids subside as you float below the Ash/Walnut Street Bridge and enter a world of fun never anticipated while traversing a river: you're now floating through the original grounds of the Ringling Brothers Barnum & Bailey Circus. *The Greatest Show on Earth* was founded in Baraboo in 1884, and you find yourself paddling by Ringling Brothers historic rail cars, trailers, buildings, and equipment stationed along both river banks. Canoeing and kayaking past a human cannon. Now how cool is that?

6 mi/1 hr 48 min: reaching the red barn on the left shore, the best route to pass the twin islands is on the far right. We've disturbed a huge (8' wing span) sandhill crane, which appears from nowhere out of the trees above us. It announces its presence with an ear-piercing prehistoric screech and is quickly out of sight, as it flies around the bend ahead.

6.2 mi/2 hrs: a fabulous class 1 rapids runs for multiple bends.

6.5 mi/2 hrs 8 min: the river flows beneath the Manchester Street Bridge, marked by two waterworks buildings along the riverbank. As a blue heron flies in low, Kenny notes that there's "no lack of excitement on this river!"

7.6 mi/2 hrs 26 min: 4 minutes from the end of your river adventure, a gorgeous stream merges from the right, flowing into the Baraboo along a natural sand and gravel seawall. This is the 14th stream or spring to merge with the river since the Manchester Rd Bridge.

7.7 mi/2 hrs 30 min: you're in! Paddle beneath the Highway 113 Bridge and take out at the boat ramp on the right.

THE TOWN: BARABOO

GREEN BAY PACKER LOCAL RADIO STATION AFFILIATE: **WBDL-FM 102.9**
MILWAUKEE BREWER LOCAL RADIO STATION AFFILIATE: **WTMJ-AM 620**

In 1837, the lure of the Baraboo River first brought European settlers to the area. Over the entire 120 mile length of the river the elevation drops 150', but through the 4 & 1/2 miles of what is now the city of Baraboo, 45' of the 150' drop occurs. This 4.5 mile stretch (from Hwy 12 in the west to Hwy 113 in the east) became known as the "Baraboo Rapids", and the power of the river's steep gradient was harnessed by the creation of five dams (all now removed), providing mechanical power to the settlers. The dams allowed grist mill and lumber mill businesses to thrive.

One popular story of how the town and river came to be called Baraboo goes like this: an 18th century French fur trapper named Baribeau ran a trading post at the confluence of (what came to be known as) the Baraboo and Wisconsin Rivers. The popularity of his trading post led to the river being named after him. What this story lacks in dash and élan is made up for in brevity and the fact that no one who was present at the time is alive to contradict it.

"The Greatest Show on Earth", the Ringling Brothers Circus, had its birth in Baraboo in 1884. The town served as Circus winter quarters for 34 years until 1918. When you float the Baraboo River just east of downtown Baraboo, you float through history: sitting along the north bank of the Baraboo River, are the original "Ringlingville" buildings. Built between 1897 and 1918, these buildings include the winter quarters office, wardrobe department, animal house (2 buildings), hippos, elephants, ring barns – stalls and practice ring, camel house, zebras, and llamas. Collectively, this is the largest surviving group of original circus structures in North America. On the south bank are the historic circus rail cars and the fabulous human cannon.

In 1907, the 5 Ringling brothers purchased the Barnum & Bailey Circus. In 1919 the two circuses were merged into one and the combined winter quarters moved from Baraboo to Bridgeport, Connecticut. Sitting on the old Baraboo site today is the "Circus World Museum", a living monument to the Ringling Brothers Circus that has been designated by the U.S. Department of Interior as a National Historic Landmark. The Circus World Museum's 64 acres includes the original "Ringlingville" buildings, is home to arguably the world's largest collection of circus artifacts, and is host to a full schedule of live circus performances from mid-May to the end of August each year.

Baraboo is home to the International Crane Foundation, founded in 1973 by 2 graduate students investigating crane behavior and ecology. The mission of the Foundation is "to commit to a future where all crane species are secure" as many of the 15 crane species are threatened, if not endangered. The ICF is the only location in the world where you can view all 15 species. They pioneered "isolation rearing", designed to allow the release of captive cranes back into the wild. The ICF has taken their mission worldwide, acting as a driving force behind projects on behalf of cranes in Africa, Russia, Cambodia, China and Vietnam. A visit to the International Crane Foundation in Baraboo allows you to view cranes in their natural habitat, among acres of restored native tall grass prairie and wetlands, and provides an opportunity to take an educational walking tour with an expert guide and learn about crane biology and conservation efforts.

A fascinating International Crane Foundation project was the reintroduction of whooping cranes to Florida by enticing a flock of whooping cranes to fly behind an ultralight aircraft flying to the sunshine state. This event may have been the inspiration behind the 1996

Jeff Daniels movie, "Fly Away Home". In the movie, a nest of goose eggs, abandoned when developers cut down a local forest, hatch and the babies are protected by a young girl who becomes their Mother Goose. The young geese, who must fly south for the winter, are led to their winter home by flying behind a pair of ultralights.

Nearby camping is available at the IDA Creek Property for a charitable contribution. The site is primitive and situated on an overlook just above the creek. Sandhill cranes, ducks, deer and other wildlife find this travel corridor just upstream from the Baraboo River between the towns of North Freedom & Baraboo near Cornfield Road & Highway 136.
Call Jon Hillmer at (608) 434-2468 or (608) 356-6048. Jon sez, "Let's have some fun, because if you aren't having fun, what are you having?"

Additional camping is at the Dell Boo Campground, between Baraboo and the Wisconsin Dells. Call (608) 356-5898 or check www.dellboo.com

THE TAVERNS: FRANKIE'S & OLD BARABOO INN

You're just getting out of the Baraboo River at the Highway 113 boat ramp and, after a long river adventure, you have a powerful thirst to quench. Well, good fortune has smiled upon you. As you leave the river access parking lot, look to your left and, just over 1/10th of a mile down Highway 113, you'll see the answer to your dry pipes sitting on the right side of the road, Frankie's. To get to Frankie's by land, follow Highway 113 southeast of Baraboo (if you pass by the Circus World Museum, you're going in the right direction).

Frankie's is a fun pub! Owner Mike Frank made 3 strangers feel right at home. He didn't blink when we asked if we could walk behind his bar, inches from his beer taps, to pose with the neon "Frankie's" sign, and even joined the out-of-towners for a commemorative photo. Mike has a real live wire of an employee in Judy, our waitress, who definitely adds to the good times at Frankie's. Since she almost broke Kenny's hand when she shook it, carrying a full tray of food and drink probably doesn't pose a problem for her.

Even the local wildlife seems to be in a hurry to get into Frankie's: the buckhead coming through the front wall indicates that there may have been a running start from across the street. The knotty-pine fun includes pool tables, darts, video machines, and out back there's horseshoe pits and volleyball courts. And, of course, Frankie's stocks Pabst Blue Ribbon beer, always a sure sign of quality!

Taking care of his customers is important to Mike. With this in mind, he provides special services that are posted on a "Bar Phone Fees" sign behind the bar. You are directed to "make arrangements with Bartender upon arrival" and Mike will answer the phone as follows when people you don't want to talk to call and ask for you…

- $1 – Not here
- $2 – On his way out
- $3 – Just Left
- $4 – Haven't seen him all day
- $5 – Who??

Frankie's, S5253 Highway 113, Baraboo WI 53913; (608) 355-9988

OLD BARABOO INN

Located in the heart of old downtown Baraboo, just south of the Baraboo River and a few steps away from Riverside Rentals, sits the Old Baraboo Inn. On the approach to the front door of my first ever visit to the Old Baraboo Inn, I was struck by the strange echo effect as I walked along the outside tavern wall on Walnut Street. The fun had just begun.

Bar owner B.C. Farr told us the fascinating story of the Old Baraboo, and it's a colorful one. The Civil War era building, once a brothel, opened around 1864. Dillinger and Capone both downed some beers and shots here. Even before those tough hombres showed their face at the Old Baraboo, this was a rough 'n tumble place, with plenty of knife fights, shootings (maybe why the "check your guns at the bar" sign is up), and good 'ole bare knuckle tussles. Folks have been killed here, which leads us to the most colorful aspect of the bar – this place is haunted. Real haunted. There's been such a large number of visitors to the bar who've witnessed some of the goings-ons that there's little doubt that paranormal activities occur, and with a good amount of frequency.

Paranormal investigators have been in and out of the bar. A few have turned tail and run, overwhelmed by the intensity of the activity. Some of the investigators are sure that what they've captured on tape are voice and sound recordings of the spirits.

Frying pans fly across the room as if hurricane-force winds blew through, flags and ashtrays, too – in the middle of the winter with the tavern sealed up tight. A 200-pound griddle has moved on its own, pictures fly off of the wall, and doors open and close by themselves. Cell phones and digital cameras go on and off and on again.

One of the shooting victims was a cowboy, a bar regular many years ago. During a bar fight, the cowboy was shot at the top of the stairs and fell back, tumbling down to the bottom of the stairway, where he died. It seems as if the cowboy is spending most of his afterlife in the Old Baraboo's basement. Going down to the basement walk-in cooler for supplies, owner B.C. and other bar employees have had the door closed behind them and the lights shut off. Now, it could be that a prank is being played, but it's happened often when the building's locked up tight and no one else is in the bar. The cowboy has also made his presence felt on the bar's main floor, once when a wedding reception was held at the bar. Two of the female wedding guests sat at the right-hand end of the bar, where there's a clear view of the kitchen. The ladies noticed a silent cowboy cooking up a big pot of beans and asked B.C. "should that cowboy be back there by the food?" When B.C. asked the ladies to point out the cowboy, he had disappeared but the pot of beans, which no one had ordered and happened to be the dead cowboy's favorite food, was still cookin' on the stove. Whew. I stood at the top of the stairs and looked down into the basement's darkness, and received a head to toes chill like nothing that I've ever felt before.

John Dombrowksi worked here for 40 years, lived in the upstairs apartment, and died in the bar. Photos taken of bar fun, many years after John died, will surprisingly include John's face and tie translucently in the background. Ladies sitting at the bar, feeling someone grab their derriere (a favorite activity of John's during his lifetime), will turn around to confront their admirer, only to find that there's no one standing there.

The upstairs apartment is available to rent for overnight stays. If you can make it 'til the morning, B.C. cooks you a no charge big breakfast to go along with your certificate that says you survived a night in the Old Baraboo Inn. Although the vast majority of folks who rent the apartment approach the evening not buying the ghost stories, or think that it'd be fun to see what happens, over half the renters are long gone well before the sun comes up. One fella who'd taken out a 6-month lease for the apartment stopped sleeping there shortly after moving in. Between the woman's voice whispering his name in his ear, and the strange tapping on the door, he decided to start spending his nighttime's on a friend's couch.

Besides being a real welcoming host, B.C. made us up some fine late night sandwiches. I heartily recommend a visit to the Old Baraboo. You may end up with your own stories to tell, and a full belly to boot. If you decide to stay overnight, you might want to sleep with the lights on. The Old Baraboo Inn, 135 Walnut Street, Baraboo WI 53913; (608) 356-2528

Sources: Jon Hillmer, Wisconsin Dept. of Natural Resources, www.riverfacts.com, Wisconsin Historical Markers, www.cityofbaraboo.com, Wikipedia, www.circusworld.wisconsinhistory.org, www.savingcranes.org

BLACK RIVER

BLACK RIVER FALLS, WI
TRIP 6.2 MILES & 2 HOURS 8 MINUTES LONG

BEGINNER ABILITY

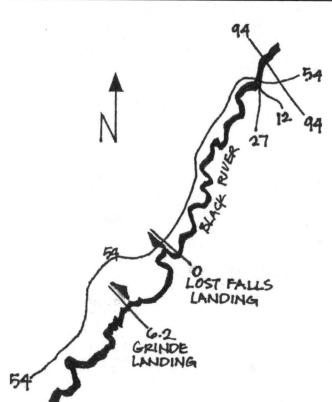

LIVERY: LOST FALLS CAMPGROUND,
N2974 SUNNYVALE ROAD
(9 MILES WEST OF BLACK
RIVER FALLS ON HWY 54),
BLACK RIVER FALLS WI
54615; (715) 284-7133
OR (800) 329-3911,
WWW.LOSTFALLS.COM
OWNERS ROSE & ED SCHAPER.

THE BACKGROUND: BLACK RIVER

SOUNDTRACK: FALL OUT – THE STAGE-MEN, THEME FROM AN IMAGINARY WESTERN – MOUNTAIN, FERRY ACROSS THE MERSEY – GERRY & THE PACEMAKERS, STATESBORO BLUES – TAJ MAHAL, TWENTY FIVE MILES – EDWIN STARR

RIVER QUOTE...
WAITRESS AT THE SUNRISE RESTAURANT IN BLACK RIVER FALLS, WHEN WE STOP FOR BREAKFAST: "MORNIN' – CAN I GET YOU A PABST?"

The stretch of the Black discussed in this chapter is found in the lower section of the river, close to the Mississippi River, where the Black is both an excellent beginner river and an excellent party river. Wide, slow, shallow and steady is the mantra, with sandy beaches (picnic/frisbee breaks) found all along the riverbanks. You are likely to enjoy eagle sightings to go with the nice rock formations viewed near the end of this stretch.

The almost 200-mile long Black River is a major tributary of the Mississippi River. The river's headwaters flow from Black Lake, about 12 miles north of Medford in north central Wisconsin. From there the Black runs southeast while passing through a series of small towns. When the Black River reaches the town of Black River Falls, it has only 50 miles left until merging with the Mississippi in Onalaska, just northwest of La Crosse.

The Black is made up of two very different parts. The Upper Black, from its beginnings at Black Lake until the dam in the town of Black River Falls, is quite rocky, much of it too rocky to paddle, and has a much faster current than below the dam, as the ground here drops 6.6 feet/mile. The Lower Black, from the Black Falls Dam downstream to the Mississippi, has a sandy bottom with a slow current as the river descends 1.7 feet/mile.

The river's dark color is caused by tannic acid emitting from the nearby tamarack & oak trees and sphagnum moss. The Ho Chunk called the water "neosheprah" meaning "dark river". 1600s French explorers named it "La Riviere Noire" meaning "The Black River".

The Black begins as a trout stream near its headwaters. Further downstream are caught walleye, northern pike, bass, muskellunge, and catfish.

The Black River canoe team was Kenny Umphrey & Doc. The trip was taken in June.

THE RIVER: PADDLING THE BLACK

Launch from the Lost Falls Campground. The river here is 2' deep and 80' wide. The depth today will vary from bottom-scraping to 3', the width from 80' to 100'. The trip ends at the Grinde Landing takeout.

The first of many wide sandy beaches is found on the first bend as the river turns left. A cabin on a high bluff across the river dominates the landscape.

.5 mi/11 min: where a creek merges from the right, you'll want to beach your boat and walk up the creek for the view. A beautiful 10' waterfall gradually flattens out as it glides down stone ledges for another 50'. The memory is worth the stop.

.7 mi/16 min: today's first island lies right of midstream. Just beyond, stairs lead up from the water on the right bank. 4 minutes later, a 25' wide & fast-moving creek merges left.

1.2 mi/28 min: a creek passes along a sandy beach on the way to merging from the left. Much of its flow is obstructed by fallen trees. Across the river on the right bank, an eagle statue guards the home beyond a long sandy beach.

1.6 mi/36 min: *"a Frisbee field!"* says Kenny. Located where a creek 5' wide at its mouth merges from the left, and where the river is 6" deep with no obstructions on the river floor, you've arrived at a great frisbee tossing spot. An eagle perches nearby to watch.

2.2 mi/49 min: reach the upstream edge of a long party beach on the left shore. The beach extends for .2 mile and 3 minutes.

2.8 mi/1 hour: higher above the water level than previous beaches, this beach on the left bank also runs for .2 mile and 3 minutes.

3.2 mi/1 hr 6 min: moving quickly and loud enough to make its presence known, a gurgling creek merges from the left. Yet another sandy beach is found on the right.

4 mi/1 hr 18 min: at the end of a long straightaway, today's biggest beach lies sprawling on the left shore, following the big bend left, and seems to fill the entire riverfront. Two very large fallen trees on the beach make fine campfire seats. Across the river on the right shore, the sand banks are 8' high.

Kenny notes that, having paddled 6 rivers in 7 days, even highly regarded *Anti-Monkey Butt Powder* might not sooth his aluminum chafing.

4.2 mi/1 hr 25 min: a creek merges from the left just before the river bends right. Along the right shore is today's highest elevation: a two-tiered beach.

4.6 mi/1 hr 36 min: at an oxbow where the river bends left, another beach lies left.

5 mi/1 hr 42 min: **stay to the right** where the river splits in order to exit the trip a little over one mile downstream at the Grinde Landing. It is important to keep right as the split in the river will not reconnect until beyond Grinde Landing.

5.4 mi/1 hr 50 min: as the river bends left, on the right bank an 8' tall rock seawall is at the base of a 25' high bluff. A beach lies cross the river.

5.7 mi/1 hr 55 min: reach the upstream end of an island; float to the right for the Grinde Landing take-out.

5.9 mi/2 hrs: on the right sits a long & high elevation beach with a 20' wide sitting log.

6 mi/2 hrs 3 min: pass by a fine looking rock outcropping as the river bends sharply left.

6.2 miles/2 hours 8 minutes: you're in! Grinde Landing take-out is on the right. A small dirt path marks the Landing.

THE TOWN: BLACK RIVER FALLS

GREEN BAY PACKER LOCAL RADIO STATION AFFILIATE: **WWIS-FM 99.7**
MILWAUKEE BREWER LOCAL RADIO STATION AFFILIATE: **WWIS-FM 99.7/WKTY-AM 580**

Jacob Spaulding arrived in the area in 1839. He was a man's man, large in size and stature. A contemporary of Spaulding's said that Jacob "met hardships and dangers as though they were but pastimes… of strong arm and unconquerable will". Upon arriving in the Black River Falls area, Jacob & his companions established a permanent settlement and built a sawmill. When supplies ran low and harsh winter weather came 'a calling, his partners left for the comfort found in big towns. Only Jacob remained at their wilderness sawmill, using his survival and hunting skills to keep safe and fed in the bitter cold. Spaulding's continued presence at the Falls during that difficult winter earned him the title, "Founder of Black River Falls".

Spaulding's bravery and ability to survive well in the wild earned him the respect of the local Native Americans, the Ho Chunk (also known as the Winnebago), a respect not given out easily or often to white men. Spaulding returned that respect and over time a deep friendship was formed between Jacob Spaulding and the original residents of the Falls area. When the federal government ordered the Ho Chunk off their ancestral lands to a reservation in Nebraska, Jacob visited the Nebraska land and decided that it was unfit for the Indians survival. Investing a great deal of his money and time, Spaulding made several trips to our nation's capital in order to find a permanent home on good land for the Ho Chunk Nation. The government men he met with tried to bribe Jacob so that he would use his influence to convince the tribal leaders to move their people to Nebraska. Jacob Spaulding replied, "I am poor, and need money badly, but you never saw money enough to induce me to be false to my Indian friends."

Spaulding took steps to spur the growth of the small settlement. He built the first hotel in the Falls, locating it on 60' of riverfront property. The hotel design & finish was regarded by all as the work of a master craftsman. In 1847, Jacob established the Falls first school, and in 1848 Black River Falls first religious services were held in his riverside hotel.

Jacob Spaulding was a man of action, of accomplishment, and of the highest character. The good folks of Black River Falls could not have a better example to follow than that of their town's founding father.

Despite Spaulding's best efforts, the people of the Ho Chunk Nation were forced to leave their Wisconsin home and resettle in Nebraska. That 1800s mistake was soon corrected, and the Ho Chunk returned home to Wisconsin after only a short time away. The Ho Chunk hold two pow-wows each year, on Memorial Day and Labor Day, in Black River Falls. All are welcome to attend this celebration of thanks and fun. Ph (715) 284-9343.

Outside of the town's founding and the return of the Ho Chunk, the biggest event in Black River Falls history was the Flood of 1911. History of the town is divided into two: "before the flood" and "after the flood". During October 1911, two weeks of heavy rainfall caused the 2 dams upstream from town, the big dam at Hatfield and the auxiliary Dells Dam, to break apart and collapse. An immense quantity of water, stored at these two dams for power purposes, was now bearing down on the Black River Falls Dam. That old dam could not hold back the water's onslaught, as now the Black River was a 1,000 foot wide channel that rolled over everything in its path. A 3-

story brick boarding house was turned upside down, the steel River Bridge was dislodged and sent downstream where it was deposited in a stand of pines. Hills were leveled and building walls were undermined, toppled over and seen floating away. A church, several residences, and 85% of the business district were no more.

But the townsfolk were resilient. 20 new brick buildings were up by the end of 1912. Typical of the enthusiasm to stay and rebuild the town were the comments of one business owner who said that he'd made his fortune in Black River Falls, he lost that fortune in the flood, and now was ready to build it there once again.

The town's rebirth included a new hydroelectric Black River Falls Dam, also built in 1912. The 1912 dam has served the town well for almost a century, but when a chunk of concrete broke off one of the flow gates in the early-2000s, the town knew it was time for a replacement dam, built in 2010 and 2011, to get them through the next 100 years.

Besides the Lost Falls Campground where the livery is located, there is camping space available on the 68,000 acres at Black River State Forest, on the eastern edge of town. The options in the Forest…

1. Castle Mound – I94 exit 116, go 1/2 mile west on Hwy 54 to Hwy 27 south then Hwy 12 east for 1 mile. There are 35 camping units with 5 electric sites and a 1.5 mile nature trail. Great view from the top of Castle Rock. Call 1-888-947-2757 for reservations.

2. East Fork – Family Camp/Group Camp/Horse Camp – I94 exit 116 to Hwy 54 east to County Rd K then left to Clay School Road then right to Campground Rd. Located on the banks of the East Fork of the Black River with a swimming beach, cross-country & hiking and riverbank nature trail. 25 camp units, 1 shelter, and the horse camp has 12 sites with tethering posts. Call 715-284-4103 or 5301.

THE TAVERN: COZY CORNER TAVERN

The Cozy Corner Tavern is located at 43 Main Street, also known as Highway 54
where Main intersects with South First Street, ph (715) 284-2651.

The first brick building erected after the Flood of 1911 was the building located at the southeast corner of Main and South First Streets, the building that today houses the Cozy Corner Tavern.

Owner Ronald Smith lets customers "pop themselves some fun" with the tavern's self- serve popcorn machine. The popcorn makes a fine appetizer to the Cozy Corner's great bar burgers and fries.

After a day floating down the Black River, you can enjoy the land-based fun offered at the Cozy Corner's darts, pool tables, and video machines.

The bar walls offer an impressive look back in time through a series of photos from the Flood of 1911, including one that says, "River Street, just before the buildings were swept away".

The impact of that Great Flood continues today through replacing the 1912 dam: workers on the 21st Century replacement dam seem to have developed a hankerin' for the Cozy's walleye fingers and drinks, a fine way to end a day building a new chapter of Black River Falls history.

Sources: Jackson County Historical Society, Jackson County Bicentennial Book, Ted Schaper, Wisconsin DNR, www.usgenney.org, *Wisconsin Builder*

BOIS BRULE RIVER

Brule, WI
Trip 12 miles & 4 hours 15 minutes long

Veteran Ability

LIVERY: BRULE RIVER CANOE RENTAL, 13869 E. US HWY. 2, BRULE WI 54820, (715) 372-4983, WWW.BRULERIVERCANOERENTAL.COM. OWNERS BRIAN, RYAN & AARON CARLSON.

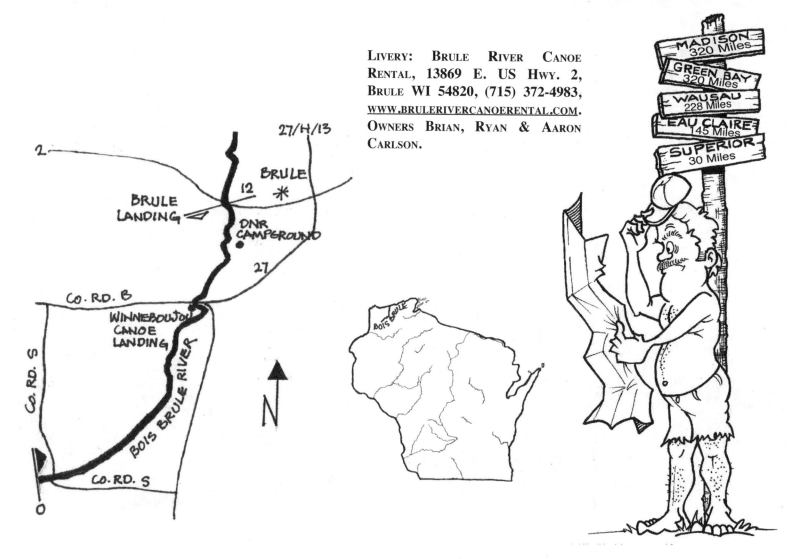

THE BACKGROUND: BOIS BRULE RIVER

SOUNDTRACK: ROCKER – THE MONTEREYS, MANNISH BOY – MUDDY WATERS, RAMBLIN' ROUND – WOODY GUTHRIE, GRANDPA BUILT BRIDGES – DANNY SCHMIDT, SIXTEEN TONS – MOBIL LOUNGE SOFTBALL TEAM & BEER SWILLERS CLUB

RIVER QUOTES...
KENNY'S VIEW OF THE BOIS BRULE:
"CANOEING AS IT OUGHTA BE"
WE ASKED A FISHERMAN IF HE'D HAD ANY BITES, "1 OR 2, BUT NOT THE SLAUGHTER WE EXPECTED".

Thirty miles southeast of the twin cities of Duluth MN and Superior WI, you'll find the beginnings of the fabulous Bois Brule River. The river flows northeast-north for 44 miles from its headwaters at the Upper St. Croix Lake until it empties into Lake Superior. The entire length of the Bois Brule flows through the 43,000 acres of the Brule State Forest. This river is as fast as it is beautiful, with a total elevation drop of 418' of which 328' takes place in the stream's last 19 miles.

This is a river that you do not want to miss. Within the 12 mile section outlined in this chapter, as the river has a 70' elevation drop, you float where President's have gone before you, through thrilling rapids runs, past gorgeous A-frame wooden bridges, see wildlife that makes you glad that you came (a photo of a Momma Merganser Duck and her 22 babies is an all-time favorite), and you are taken back in time as you paddle next to century-old Adirondack-style riverside homes.

The Bois Brule is a river that you can paddle any time of the year, and know that there will be sufficient water to float your canoe or kayak. This river is fed by so many springs that a constant river depth is maintained year round.

The Bois Brule is known as the "River of Presidents", having been visited by 5 Presidents beginning with Ulysses S. Grant, Grover Cleveland (as baseball fans can relate to, it's very hard not to type in "Alexander" after his name), Calvin Coolidge, Herbert Hoover, and Dwight David Eisenhower. The first lodges along the river were built in preparation for Grant's 1870s visit. These Presidents came to fish in this legendary trout stream.

The Bois Brule River flows north in the former channel of a much larger river that once flowed south. That earlier channel was carved at the end of the Ice Age, from the melting ice that surged south from the shrinking glacial Lake Duluth (part of what is now Lake Superior). As the glaciers receded over time, a divide was formed in which the Bois Brule and the St. Croix Rivers flow in opposite directions. Instead of flowing southward out of Lake Superior, the Bois Brule now flows northward into the Big Lake. The Bois Brule and St. Croix Rivers, linked by Upper St. Croix Lake, have been used for centuries as the water highway connecting Lake Superior to the Mississippi River.

Paddling the Bois Brule were Kenny Umphrey and Doc. The trip took place in June.

THE RIVER: PADDLING THE BOIS BRULE

Launch at the Stones Bridge Canoe Landing (complete with restrooms) at Highway S, and take out at the Highway 2 Canoe Landing (also complete with restrooms) on the left just before Hwy. 2.

As you launch, the river is 25' wide, 2' deep, and there are stones everywhere, giving the landing its name. In the early going, rocks in the river are placed from left shore to right in such a way that chutes are formed to float through midstream.

1 mi/23 min: the river has receded to 1' deep and widen to 70' across. Downstream, trees leaning in from both shores seem to reach up towards the sky.

1.8 mi/42 min: a creek merges from the right with pilings near its mouth. The river is 50' across and 2' deep.

2 mi/48 min: as the river bends left, a sign on the right shore reads, "Private Land beyond this point. Please do not camp or litter. DNR campground 10 miles".

2.2 mi/52 min: lagoon is on the left; 1/10th mile downstream, an island lies at the point where a dead creek merges from the left.

2.7 mi/1 hr 2 min: reach the upstream edge of a large island (w/ 40' tall trees), plenty of water to pass either left or right. At the downstream tip of the island, a creek merges left.

3.3 mi/1 hr 18 min: there's a small island left of midstream as the river bends right.

3.6 mi/1 hr 25 min: at the upstream end of a long island, pass either left or right. At the island's end, you've reached the boathouse of the Cedar Island Estate. The first buildings on the estate were built in the early-1900s. Calvin Coolidge stayed at the Estate so long in the summer of 1928 that the national press called it the "summer White House". Coolidge had decided not to run for re-election that fall, and hosted Presidential candidate Herbert Hoover here. Dwight Eisenhower stayed at the Estate while on a trout fishing expedition in 1947, and returned again during his '52 to 60' White House years. Viewed within and adjacent to the Cedar Island Estate, are several more beautiful homes that you'll paddle by over the next few minutes.

3.8 mi/1 hr 30 min: a midstream island has footbridges that you can paddle beneath on both the island's right and left.

3.9 mi/1 hr 33 min: flow through the first of many whitewater runs that you see today. Although this run is short in duration, it elicits a "*whee!!!*" from a paddler as you fly through a chute created by stone walls both right and left.

4 mi/1 hr 35 min: as the river bends right, a pretty little class 1 run flows beneath a footbridge.

4.1 mi/1 hr 37 min: an island is encountered; the wider opening flows to the island's left, but on the right and flowing beneath a footbridge

is a fun rapids run through a 10' wide chute.

4.5 mi/1 hr 47 min: you're into the start of *Fall Rapids*. After paddling through a 100' wide and shallow bay, you hear the loud rapids ahead as the river tightens to 12' wide. This is an exciting run with a mix of class 1 and 2 rapids. Stay to the right or the large rocks midstream will getcha! You barely have time to catch your breath, and you're flying through *Big Twin Rapids*, class 1 rapids fun through some big waves.

4.9 mi/1 hr 53 min: coming out of a 70' wide bay, the river narrows to 15' and *Little Twin Rapids* is upon you; this run is a two-minute long class 1 and 2 mix, ending at a wide and a shallow bay (seems to be a pattern developing here). Challenging and fun!

5.4 mi/2 hrs 4 min: reaching the upstream edge of a long field of cattails, you're entering the first of two lakes known as "Big Lake", an estimated 150' wide.

5.8 mi/2 hrs 14 min: the lake narrows back to a 30' wide river as you approach a boathouse on the right bank. Two bends downstream, a very cool "rock dock" extends 12' into the river from the right shore.

5.9 mi/2 hrs 17 min: a minute long class 1 run known as *Wildcat Rapids* connects the Big Lake to the second of two lakes, Lucius Lake.

6 mi/2 hrs 19 min: reach the upstream edge of an island guarded by reeds and cattails and the start of Lucius Lake.

6.5 mi/2 hrs 28 min: Lucius Lake narrows back to a river as you approach a boathouse on the left shore.

6.6 mi/2 hrs 32 min: river bends right, and you paddle through a tight opening between trees leaning in from each shore. Just beyond is a footbridge.

7 mi/2 hrs 41 min: at the end of a long straight away sits a home with _really_ nice stairs leading down to the river; as the rivers then bends left there's a boathouse on the right.

7.4 mi/2 hrs 48 min: looking down a long straight away, you see at its end a beautiful off- white wood boathouse where the river bends left. The boathouse fronts a grand log home on higher ground.

7.6 mi/2 hrs 55 min: far & away the trip's finest Frisbee area, as the Bois Brule bends right. It's 70' across, 2' deep, with a firm sandy bottom free of river floor obstructions & running 200' long.

7.9 mi/3 hrs: you come upon a log fallen from the left bank, almost reaching the right bank, and lying 3' above the water surface; 100' downstream float beneath a footbridge.

8 mi/3 hrs 2 min: on the left shore is a beautiful boathouse with a shaded gable; a fine home sits just beyond it as the river turns to the right.

8.3 mi/3 hrs 8 min: *Station Rapids* is a light riffles run for 3 bends which then becomes a class 1 rapids run for the next 3 minutes.

8.7 mi/3 hrs 15 min: Winneboujou Canoe Landing, with restrooms, is on the left shore. Highway B is visible just downstream.

8.8 mi/3 hrs 16 min: immediately after passing beneath the Highway B Bridge, enter the *Williamson Rapids*. This rapids runs 5 minutes and .3 of a mile. We were bouncing off of more rocks than we could count. A spirited river stretch!

At the end of this 5 minute run, the river current slows for 5 minutes.

9.2 mi/3 hrs 25 min: the *Hall Rapids* run begins, another 5 minutes and .3 of a mile of fun! What begins as a class 1 rapids becomes a great class 2 adventure!

10 mi/3 hrs 40 min: back-to-back partial beaver dams are encounter, the first on a left bend and the second on a right bend. One bend downstream from the 2nd beaver dam, you begin a two-minute class 1 & 2 rapids run known as the *Long Nebagamon Rapids*.

10.6 mi/3 hrs 45 min: *Little Joe Rapids*, a brief and wild class 2 run that lasts for 1 straight away. The river drops 6' in 40 yards! Stay to the right! *Big* rocks lie midstream and to the left.

10.8 mi/3 hrs 50: Bois Brule Campground is along the right shore. It may be reached on land by driving south from Highway 2 for one mile on Ranger Road. There are 20 sites available, 17 pull-in and 3 walk-in. Call (715) 372-5678.
There are two more nice class 1+ runs over the next ten minutes.

12 miles/4 hours & 15 minutes: you're in! The Highway 2 Canoe Landing, with restrooms, is on your left and just before the Highway 2 Bridge.

THE TOWN: BRULE

Green Bay Packer local radio station affiliate: WNXR-FM 107.3
Milwaukee Brewer local radio station affiliate: WIKB-FM 99.1

Brule is a small town of 600 or so residents, located 15 miles north of the boundary between the Lake Superior watershed and the Mississippi River watershed. Brule was settled on November 13, 1886, along the Northern Pacific Railroad line (now the Tri-County Corridor Trail). As does the Bois Brule River, the town lies within the 43,000 acres of the Brule River State Forest.

The Brule River State Forest began with a 4,000 acre gift given in 1907 to the state of Wisconsin by Frederick Weyerhauser, a self-made man who made his fortune in land acquisition. As 1899 became 1900, he owned more timberland than any other person in America. Weyerhauser also showed more concern for his workers than any other industrialist of his time, and he made sure that each of those workers understood the importance of even the smallest of trees. To those who knew Frederick, his generous 4,000 acre gift to the state was very much in character. This 4,000 acre gift was supplemented by state land purchases over the years until the State Forest reached its current 43,000 acres. 16 miles of the North Country National Scenic Trail, a 4,600 mile footpath linking North Dakota to New York, passes through the Brule River State Forest.

Brule is situated in the northeastern section of Douglas County. Douglas County is also home to the town of Superior WI who, along with her sister city of Duluth MN, forms the leading bulk cargo port on the Great Lakes.

America's all-time leading air ace, Major Dick Bong, was born 11 miles west of Brule in Poplar, WI. Dick joined the Army Air Corps in 1942 and went on to shoot down 40 Japanese aircraft in World War II. The Congressional Medal of Honor was awarded to Bong in December 1944, and General Douglas McArthur cited the young Wisconsin air ace as entering the "society of the bravest of the brave". "America's Ace of Aces" lost his life testing a jet plane in August 1945 and is buried in his hometown.

THE TAVERN: THE KRO BAR & GRILL

THE KRO BAR & GRILL IS LOCATED ON US HIGHWAY 2 IN BRULE, PHONE (715) 327-4876.

The Kro Bar is a fine old knotty pine bar located on US Highway 2, just west of Hwy 27 and a few minutes down the street from the Brule River Canoe Rental. It was the good fortunate of Kenny and me to arrive at the Kro Bar in the middle of their Friday night fish fry. These folks *do* fix some great walleye! It turns out that walleye goes especially well with Pabst Blue Ribbon beer. A Sunday morning breakfast special of Bloody Marys and biscuits 'n gravy was posted on the wall. Now we're talkin'!

A good-sized crowd was on hand, as you would expect on a Friday night, and they were entertained with live music in the side room. Besides the music, there's plenty to keep you occupied at the Kro Bar with darts, ping pong, pool tables, quite a few video games, a juke box, and large screen TVs.

Maybe the greatest photo in Packer history adorns a Kro Bar wall. It's a picture of the 1962 World Championship team. Instead of the usual grim-faced official team look, in this photo the guys are giggling, hugging, posing cross-eyed, and generally engaged in some good old tom foolery. I'm guessing that Coach Lombardi was absent on this day. Hysterical!

On the Kro Bar walls were framed pictures of five different outdoor scenes, each scene with a Pabst Blue Ribbon border. We're home Auntie Em!

Sources: Brule River State Forest Visitor, www.midwestweekends.com, Paddling Northern Wisconsin – Mike Svob, Exploring Wisconsin Trout Streams – Born, www.wisconsinpaddleguide.com, Wisconsin DNR, www.germanheritage.com, www.northcountrytrail.org, Brule Country – Albert Marshall, Brian Carlson

THE BRULE RIVER

FLORENCE, WI
TRIP **6.7** MILES & **2** HOURS LONG

INTERMEDIATE ABILITY

LIVERY: NORTHWOODS WILDERNESS OUTFITTERS, N-4088 PINE MOUNTAIN ROAD, IRON MOUNTAIN MI 49801, (906) 774-9009, WWW.NORTHWOODSOUTFITTERS. COM. OWNERS CINDY AND RANDY "GUS" GUSTAFSON. IN ADDITION TO THE BRULE RIVER, NORTHWOODS SERVICES THE MENOMINEE, THE PINE, & THE MICHIGAMME RIVERS.

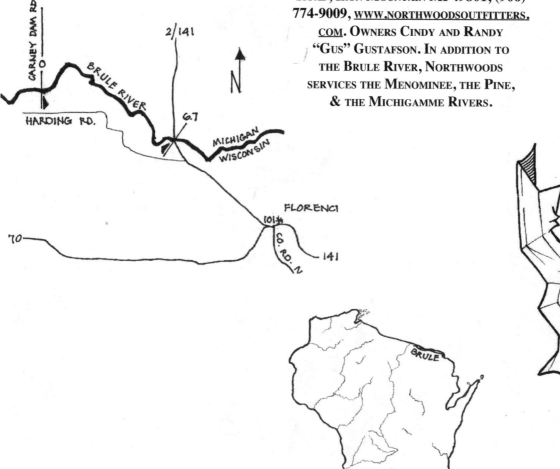

BRULE RIVER

SOUNDTRACK: LIQUORED UP & LACQUERED DOWN – DESPERATE OTTOS, RAIN IS A GOOD THING – LUKE BRYAN, I NEVER THOUGHT I'D LIVE TO BE A MILLION – MOODY BLUES, LOVELY RITA – THE BEATLES, GREAT FILLING STATION HOLDUP – JIMMY BUFFETT,

RIVER QUOTES…
RANDY GUSTAFSON: "I'VE NEVER PUT ANYONE IN WHO'S FLIPPED ON THIS STRETCH OF THE RIVER"
KENNY ON TIPPING: 'THERE'S THOSE THAT HAVE, AND THOSE THAT WILL"

In the extreme northeastern corner of Wisconsin, you'll find the 53-mile long Brule River. The Brule has its headwaters at the bottom of Brule Lake, just north of the small town of Nelma, Wisconsin. From there, the Brule River flows east, forming the border between northern Wisconsin and the southern edge of Michigan's Upper Peninsula. The Brule comes to an end at its junction with the Michigamme River, 5 minutes northeast of Florence, Wisconsin and 15 minutes northwest of Iron Mountain, Michigan. The Brule & Michigamme confluence forms the beginning of the Menominee River.

The occasional riffle, rapids, and rock garden make this a river best suited for folks who know how to use a paddle to steer a canoe or a kayak. Beginners should only float with an experienced hand in the back of the boat.

On our ride to our Brule launch site, livery owner Randy shared some river info with us:

• His customers report 5 or 6 bear sightings each year along the Brule.
• By June 2010, the river was at its lowest level in 67 years, & then the rains came.
• On our trip, the Brule was running at 330 cfps (cubic feet per second). To ensure that Randy's customers have enough water to actually float (versus walk) their boat downstream, 200 is the cfps minimum that Randy will put folks on the river at. During the first week of June 2010 (the previously noted "lowest point in 67 years"), the cfps was 142.
• On today's stretch (Carney Road to US2), when there is an equal flow left and right around an island, there will be fewer obstructions met by going right. This is the rule for every island encountered except the final island, the one just past the train trestle. At this island, it is important to stay left! This is a _significant_ caveat to remember.
• The Brule is a great brook & brown trout stream.
•Among Randy's most memorable customers: a local man was dating a French lady who had a girlfriend visiting from her home country. Along with another local guy, the group rented canoes from Northwoods to paddle the Brule. The girls went down to the river while the boys unloaded the canoes. By the time the guys got down to the river's edge, the girls were topless, eliciting a "no, no, no" from the men. There's much that we can learn from the French.

The Brule Paddling Team was Toni Laporte, Paul Pienta, Kenny Umphrey, Tommy Holbrook, Maggie & Doc. We floated the Brule in June.

THE RIVER: PADDLING THE BRULE

Launch at the Carney Dam Road, 1 mile off Prairie Acres Road, and take out beneath the US2 Bridge at the Wisconsin-Michigan state line, 4 miles northwest of Florence.

The Brule is 40' wide as you launch. The river depth varies from bottom scraping to 2'.

.6 mi/10 min: arrive at the base of a high right bluff, upon where a metal-roofed large log cabin & a guest house sits.

1.2 mi/20 min: the Brule wraps around the river bank to the right, and into the start of a nice class 1 rapids run.

1.4 mi/26 min: you're into a two-bend riffle run.

1.7 mi/30 min: reach the upstream edge of multiple midstream islands, ending with a house on a left bluff.

2.4 mi/40 min: a pretty little log cabin sits on the right shore. The river rain is turning Pabst into Hamm's.

3.7 mi/1 hour: on the left bank is a two-story house with a cinder block lower level.

4.1 mi/1 hr 7 min: you float in light rapids through a rock garden.

4.5 mi/1 hr 15 min: enter two-minute long "pinball rapids" (per Maggie), a run of light class one rapids.

How quickly life can change on the river…
At the beginning of these light rapids,
without warning, a 35' tall tree falls across
the Brule, missing Kenny & Tommy by
about 50'.

5 mi/1 hr 20 min: at an island lying right of
midstream, a very fast current with rapids
flows 200 yards around the island's right.

5.7 mi/1 hr 38 min: dead creek merges
from the right.

5.9 mi/1 hr 42 min: big island right, little
island left.

6 mi/1 hr 43 min: float beneath the tall train
trestle. Remember that when you reach the
next island, for the first (and only) time
today, stay left and NOT right.

6.4 mi/1 hr 50 min: you've now reached
that next island – *STAY LEFT!* At the
upstream end of the island, a large house
is on the right shore. The flow to the right
around this island is frequently thick
with obstructions *plus* there are sections
where the water is over your head. Paul
& Toni flipped their canoe here and found
themselves righting their boat in water
6' deep with an overgrown shoreline that
would not allow a foothold.

6.7 miles/2 hours: you're in! Float beneath
the US2 Bridge, exiting the river left under
the bridge.

THE TOWN: FLORENCE

Green Bay Packer local radio station affiliate: WCYE-FM 93.7
Milwaukee Brewer local radio station affiliate: WCYE-FM 93.7

The town of Florence is the county seat for Florence County. Florence Hulst was the first white woman to settle in the area, and the town and county are named in her honor. This is an area that offers a wide variety of ways to enjoy nature: paddle the rivers serviced by Northwoods Wilderness Outfitters and quite a bit beyond as there are 265 lakes and 165 miles of streams in the county, hike 15 signed trails, bike along 5 mountain trails in addition to various popular road routes, snowmobile 180 groomed miles, ski Keyes Peak, and visit the beauty of the Nicolet National Forest. 80% of Florence County is forested, offering great opportunities for Fall color tours. Take time to view the 7 waterfalls in the county (3 on the Pine River and 4 on the Popple River). The *Wild Rivers Interpretive Center* is located on

the western edge of the town of Florence at the corner of Highways 2 and 70, and is a wonderful resource for planning a waterfall tour, as well as to answer any other question you may have about the great outdoors of Florence County.

There are no stoplights in Florence County. What a wonderful thought, one that takes you back to another time. Florence has the 2nd lowest population of Wisconsin's 72 counties with a little over 5,000 residents. The area was home to fur trappers and hunters until the late-1860s when loggers uncovered the majestic white pines. After the discovery of iron ore in 1873, the Menominee River Railway was built to support the mining operations, and served to open up the area to the outside world.

Logging came to an end in the area in the early-1900s after the loggers exhausted the pine and decimated the hardwoods and hemlock. In stark contrast to the "scorched earth" policy of the European timber men stood the Menominee Native Americans and their leader, Chief Oshkosh. Before his death in 1856, Oshkosh directed his people to harvest their forest gradually from one side of their reservation to the other. This method allowed each timber stand the time required to renew itself and to provide a long-term source of timber for the Menominee.

The history of industry in Florence County took a turn in the 1920s-1940s that certainly sounds strange now. There was a big time prostitution ring operating in Florence County back then, centered 7 minutes east of the town of Florence in the community of Spread Eagle. There are several tasteless jokes that come to mind (to quote Glen Quagmire, "giggity giggity"). Many of the girls were tricked into the business by being offered good paying jobs that did not exist, and then kidnapped from Chicago or Milwaukee and brought to northern Wisconsin. Most of the activity occurred at a place called the Hollywood Hotel. Ironically the Hotel's letterhead proclaimed it "A fine place, just like home". Spread Eagle law enforcement would be paid off by the brothel owners and look the other way – until a payment was missed and they would conduct a raid. Men would visit the brothel during hunting season, and pay kids to shoot a deer and strap it to their cars for the ride home. An increase in the presence of state law enforcement agents finally stopped the trade in the late-1940s.

A warm & welcoming place for Florence lodging is the Lakeside Bed & Breakfast. The Lakeside is owned by the charming Rita, and built by her dear, late husband Ronny. As you approach town from the east, on a big US2 bend, you'll find the Lakeside. The rooms on the 2nd floor facing south provide you with a fabulous view of Fisher Lake. Each room has its own TV, fireplace (nice), and bathroom. And then there's breakfast. Breakfast served by candlelight. Breakfast served with dessert. In our crack research group, some members not known for carelessly flinging praise about were downright giddy in their reviews of the Lakeside breakfast. Lovely Rita has the perfect, warm personality to run a B&B. We will be back. And we were.

Florence area camping is available at several locations, the nearest at Lake Emily, 3 miles south of town on County Road D, east of Highway 101 and west of County Road N. For a complete listing of local camping, pick up a "Pine-Popple Wild Rivers" map from the Wild Rivers Interpretive Center.

THE TAVERN: THE FILLING STATION

I like this place. Pabst on tap, Pabst in longnecks, or Pabst in cans. Do a little dance, drink a little Pabst, get down tonight. Baby.

The Filling Station is a short walk down the street from Rita's Lakeside Bed & Breakfast.
Owner Ron pours your buyer-friendly sized shots at your table, right in front of you. A little nicety, letting you know that you're not getting stiffed, just stiff.

Video games, pool tables, and darts are available, if you like. The Filling Station sound track is loud rock & roll, so be prepared. If you hang in the back of the bar, the music goes right through you, but in the front of the bar you can sit and talk without yelling.

The previous owner died while working behind the bar. Upon hearing this piece of information, Kenny commented, "Talk about the captain going down with the ship!"

That's when we first saw the bear… there's a very big bear skin splayed out on the wall near the bar's front entrance. It's a nice fit with the other bare décor.

Cause for concern: on the wall by the bear skin is a sign for "diet whiskey, 1/3rd fewer calories – less alcohol, fewer calories". Sounds like a trade Detroit Lions management would make. Diet whiskey? Isn't that the first sign of the apocalypse?

The Filling Station burgers are getting rave reviews at our table. Maggie, how's yours? Answer (with nodding head & smiling eyes): *ooo!!!* There's excellent food here. When Tommy praises the "toasty buns", he's not talking 'bout the photos of gals on the walls (maybe I should confirm that with him). We were informed that the chef for these fine culinary creations is Nor, or Ron spelled backwards. You don't question genius; you just ask that the grub keeps on coming.

The Filling Station is located at 740 Central Avenue, phone (715) 528-5898.

Sources: Randy Gustafson, Northwoods Wilderness Outfitters, www.wistravel.com, www.wisconsinpaddleguide.com, Wild Rivers Interpretive Center, History of Florence County to 1890, Voyageurs magazine

CHICAGO RIVER

CHICAGO IL
TRIP 5.3 MILES & 1 HOURS 42 MINUTES LONG

INTERMEDIATE ABILITY

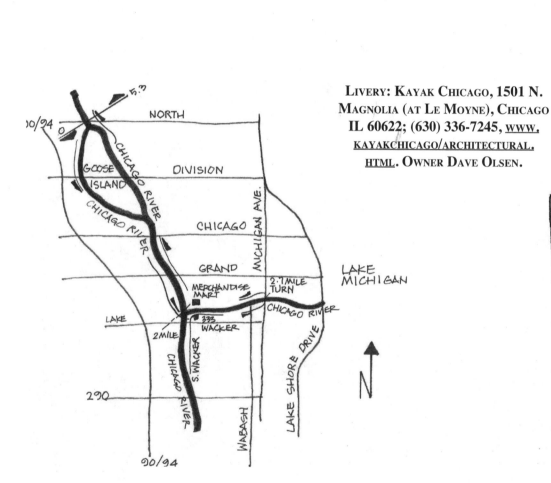

LIVERY: KAYAK CHICAGO, 1501 N. MAGNOLIA (AT LE MOYNE), CHICAGO IL 60622; (630) 336-7245, WWW. KAYAKCHICAGO/ARCHITECTURAL. HTML. OWNER DAVE OLSEN.

CHICAGO RIVER

SOUNDTRACK: A DYING CUB FAN'S LAST REQUEST/LINCOLN PARK PIRATES – STEVE GOODMAN, WANG DANG DOODLE – KOKO TAYLOR, SING, SING, SING – BENNY GOODMAN (FEATURING GENE KRUPA), HEY BARTENDER – BLUES BROTHERS, YOU DON'T HAVE TO GO – MUDDY WATERS (LIVE AT MISTER KELLY'S)

RIVER QUOTE...
PEGGY: "PETER CRIED WHEN (HIS DAUGHTER) KELLY PASSED THE BAR."
VID: "CAUSE HE THOUGHT SHE'D BOUGHT A BAR"

The Chicago River flows for 156 miles including the North Branch, the South Branch, & the Main Stem which run east to west and connects the river to Lake Michigan. The river system features 52 miles of constructed waterways including the North Shore Channel, the Sanitary & Ship Canal, and the Calumet Sag Channel.

Until the late-1800s, the North Branch flowed south, the South Branch flowed north, and they met at the western end of the Main Stem, near where the Merchandise Mart is today. At the confluence of the 3 branches is an area known as Wolf Point, the initial European settlement in Chicago. From here, the river flowed east through the marshes and wetlands of the Main Stem and on into Lake Michigan.

These flow patterns changed in the late-1800s. To stop the dumping of untreated Chicago River industrial waste into Lake Michigan, the main source of drinking water for city residents (and to stop cholera & typhoid fever outbreaks), a major engineering project took place. The flow of the Main Stem of the Chicago River was reversed so that the river flowed away from Lake Michigan (by digging a channel through a ridge on the city's west edge, and using gravity and the landscape's natural plane). The North Branch of the river continued its original flow south merging with the now westbound current of the Main Stem at Wolf Point. From there, the Chicago River now flowed south down its South Branch and into the Sanitary & Ship Canal, which emptied into the Des Plaines River and ultimately into the Mississippi River. It was believed that the mighty flows of both the Des Plaines and the Mississippi Rivers would dilute the Chicago River waste to harmless levels. This engineering feat was not greeted joyously in those communities downriver from Chicago.

Today, reclaiming the health of the Chicago River is heading in the right direction, but a great deal of work is still needed. Advisories remain about eating the fish (smallmouth, largemouth & rock bass, carp, bluegill, catfish) caught in the river. Working to restore the health of the river is the environmental group Friends of the Chicago River. Formed in 1979, they work with governments, businesses and private residents to reduce river waste and clean up the water system. The Friends efforts include rebuilding riverbanks and wetlands, and restoring the river's original habitat. See www.chicagoriver.org.

The Chicago River trip discussed in this chapter takes you south on the North Branch to Wolf Point, from there heading east on the Main Stem towards Lake Michigan. At the Wabash Avenue Bridge, you turn around and retrace your steps to the launch site. To get the most out of our Chicago River adventure, we floated with the crew at Kayak Chicago. Dave Olsen's team kayaks alongside you, while sharing their knowledge of the river, the area's history, and the riverside architecture in an entertaining and informative way.

Paddling the river was the Chicago 20: Lindsey & Don Rogers, Phyllis & Pat Kennedy, Megan Beuthin, Scott Manley, Bernadette Kearns, Ellen Kalwitz, Pete & Peggy & Kelly Armstrong, Mary Pat Sampsell, Arlene Angert, Vid Marvin, Nathan Garcia, Ania Majewska-Garcia, Paula Brown, Andy & Bob Kocembo, and Doc.

THE RIVER: PADDLING THE CHICAGO

Launch from the Kayak Chicago dock at the turning basin on the North Branch of the Chicago River, just south of the North Avenue Bridge. The trip ends at this same spot.

The trip begins on the northern edge of man-made Goose Island. You will paddle south on the North Branch of the Chicago River. Stay to the right in order to go down the west side of Goose Island (you'll return on the island's east side). The current here is with you.

.3 mi/7 min: paddle beneath the Division Street Bridge. A few feet before the bridge, you see the Morton Salt plant on the right. Ironically, earlier today when it rained it poured.

.9 mi/19 min: Kendall College is on the left. Established in 1934, Kendall relocated in 2005 from the suburbs to a restored, century-old factory building on Goose Island.

1 mi/22 min: float beneath the Halsted Street Bridge.

1.1 mi/24 min: reach the downstream edge of Goose Island. The original Montgomery Ward Distribution Center is on the left.

1.2 mi/27 min: float below the Chicago Avenue Bridge. The Green Door Tavern (see "Taverns" section of the chapter) is 5 blocks east (left) and 2 blocks south of here.

1.5 mi/33 min: pass beneath the Ohio Street Bridge.

1.6 mi/35 min: reach the Grand Avenue Bridge.

1.8 mi/39 min: paddle beneath the Kinzie Street Bridge. Beyond the bridge and to the left is the Chicago Sun-Times. You're beginning to see the buildings that make up the great downtown Chicago canyons.

Kinzie Street side note: in 2004 the Dave Matthews Band reached an added level of notoriety while crossing over this bridge while on tour. A sight seeing boat was passing below the Kinzie Bridge as the Band's bus drove over the bridge's metal grates. The bus driver at that moment pushed a button which emptied the bus' septic tank & its 80 to 100 gallon's of human waste on to the boat and its 120 passengers. A direct hit was made on those sitting on the boat's upper deck. Shortly after the vomiting and general nausea, the lawsuits were filed. Interestingly, the Dave Matthews Band was playing Wrigley Field the weekend that we paddled with Kayak Chicago. We were careful not to follow the band's lyrics to "look up at the sky", just in case, as we floated below the Kinzie Bridge.

2 mi/42 min: you reach the confluence of the 3 branches of the river, as the North Branch comes to an end. To the left is the Main Stem and the South Branch is ahead and to the right. Among the buildings at the confluence of these 3 branches…

- Visible looking down South Branch and on the west (right) shore is the Boeing International World HQ.
- The curved green glass facade of 333 West Wacker Building is along the Main Stem of the river, at the southeast corner of where the 3 branches meet (as you turn on to the Main Stem, on your right). 333 West Wacker also served as Ferris Bueller's father's office in the 1986 classic movie *Ferris Bueller's Day Off*.
- Across the Main Stem from 333 West Wacker, on your left, is the Merchandise Mart. With 4,000,000 feet of floor space, only the Pentagon is bigger worldwide.

Follow the bend to the left to begin paddling down the Main Stem of the Chicago River, taking you towards Lake Michigan. Although you are floating against the current, it's not noticeable.

2.2 mi/45 min: float beneath the Franklin Street Bridge. The Chicago Riverwalk is on the right (south) bank and runs east to Lake Michigan. The Merchandise Mart is on your left and 333 West Wacker is on your right.

2.3 mi/47 min: arrive at the Wells Street Bridge.

2.4 mi/48 min: paddle below the LaSalle Street Bridge.

2.45 mi/50 min: Clark Street Bridge.
2.5 mi/51 min: Dearborn Street Bridge. On the left shore is the House of Blues.

2.6 mi/52 min: pass the marina on the left and arrive at the State Street Bridge. Beyond the bridge and to the right is a wonderful piece of Gothic architecture known as 35 East Wacker. It was built in 1926 and known as the Jewelers Building. For the safety of the diamond merchants who did business here, and avoid muggings between their offices and their cars, an auto elevator was installed that would rise to the 22nd floor. The merchants could drive into the building and take the elevator to the floor where they worked. The elevators were eventually remodeled into additional offices. During Prohibition, the space just under the dome was used as a speakeasy by Al Capone.

2.7 mi/54 min: reach the Wabash Avenue Bridge. On the left bank is the Trump Tower and just to its east is the Wrigley Building. From here, turn your boats around & retrace your steps back to Kayak Chicago. On the Main Stem, and with your back to Lake Michigan, the current is now with you.

Just beyond the Franklin Street Bridge, you'll arrive back at Wolf Point. Follow the river as it bends right & enter the North Branch. You're now paddling against the mild current.

4.1 mi/1 hr 20 min: reach the downstream end of Goose Island. Stay to the right to get the east view of the island (at the beginning, you came down the west side).

5.3 mi/1 hr 42 min: at the dock of Kayak Chicago, you're in!

THE TOWN: CHICAGO

Chicago White Sox radio station: WSCR-AM 670
Chicago Cubs radio station: WGN-AM 720
Chicago Bears radio station: WBBM-AM 780

Late one night, when we were all in bed,
Mrs. O'Leary lit a lantern in the shed.
Her cow kicked it over,
Then winked her eye and said,
"There'll be a hot time in the old town tonight!"

Anywhere in the United States, from school children to old timers, folks can tell you about Mrs. O'Leary's cow and the Great Chicago Fire of 1871. There was another Chicago event, one not often recalled today, but one that in its time was considered to be as transformative to our country as the Revolutionary War or the Civil War. That event was the 1893 World's Columbian Exposition, commonly known as the Great Chicago World's Fair or also *the White City*.

The 1893 World's Fair was advertised as a way to commemorate the 400th anniversary of the discovery of America by Christopher Columbus. The true driving force behind the Fair though, was the wildly successful 1889 "Exposition Universelle" held in Paris. This 1889 Fair was called "the most marvelous exhibit of modern times, or ancient times". The magnifique centerpiece of the Paris World's Fair was the Eiffel Tower, rising into the sky at 1,000 feet, the tallest man-made structure on earth. Suddenly, the engineering feats of the United States paled in comparison to this Old World achievement, and the feeling swept the country that we needed to top the French (or "out-Eiffel the Eiffel"). Chicago was chosen as the city that we would hold our Fair in and regain our leading international position in. Our Fair would be the greatest such event ever held. To properly frame this historic event, the location picked in Chicago would be near the water, along Chicago's beautiful asset, Lake Michigan, but not before a great debate ensued.

Frederick Law Olmstead designed the landscape on which the Fair would be held. He was the best in the world at his craft, considered the Father of American Landscape Architecture, and his famous work included designing the grounds of New York's Central Park, the Asheville, N.C. Vanderbilt Estate, and Detroit's Belle Isle. Olmstead's argument for the Jackson Park site along Lake Michigan won the day as he noted that, "Many visitors, until they arrive here, will have never seen a broad body of water extending to the horizon; will never have seen a vessel under sail, nor a steamboat of half the tonnage of those seen hourly passing in and out of the Chicago harbor; and will never have seen such effects of reflected light or of clouds piling up from the horizon, as are to be enjoyed every summer's day on the lake margin of the city."

Olmstead's landscape complimented structures designed & built by the leading architects and engineers in the country. Almost all the Fair's buildings were of neoclassical design (their columns and pediments evoking the glories of ancient Rome), each covered with plaster of Paris, and painted a chalky white, thus earning the Fair the name "White City".

The 1893 World's Columbian Exposition lasted for 6 months, from May to October. The Expo brought in 27.5 million visitors, when our total population measured 65 million (imagine an event today drawing 125 million folks, the equivalent of 250 Woodstocks or

5,000 Canoecopias). The 1893 Fair remains to this day the most heavily attended entertainment event in the world. In a time of poor mass communication, word of mouth spread across the world with incredible speed, begun from visitors amazed at the Fair's grandeur, beauty, and innovation…

•	The Fair's largest structure was the *Manufacturers and Liberal Arts Building*. In the build-up to the Fair, promoters tried to get people enthusiastic about the size of the building by talking about the enormous amount of steel, iron, etc., that went into its construction. It wasn't until it was suggested that the building was "large enough to house the entire standing Russian Army" that the oohs and aahs began. Nobody really knew what that meant except something really big and the Russian Army analogy was repeated in every America town. Today, we could say it was big enough to house 5 Lambeau Fields (the playing field, stands and concessions included).

•	Entire villages from around the world were on display (ex: African villages, "Streets of Cairo", etc.) on the Fair's Midway. The sensation of the Midway's belly dancers drew the men folk in very, very large numbers.

•	How did we "out Eiffel the Eiffel?" With the Fair introducing the world to the Ferris Wheel, invented by George Ferris. This first ever Ferris Wheel took riders 264' into the sky above the fairgrounds, in 36 boxes each the size of a railroad car (weighing thirteen tons apiece, not including passengers) & each box with enough room to hold 60 people. It took 20 minutes for one complete revolution of the wheel. Eight 140' tall towers were needed to support the Ferris Wheel's giant axle. The wheel itself remains today the largest single-piece casting ever made.

•	Fair buildings were painted not by a brush, but through a hose with a nozzle created from a piece of gas pipe – the world's first spray paint.

•	The dedication of the Fair was an event that was met with excitement all over America. Francis J. Bellamy thought an excellent idea would be if school kids everywhere joined in a chorus of support, and he wrote a pledge for them to read. The Federal Bureau of Education sent a copy to virtually every school in the country of Bellamy's composition, *the Pledge of Allegiance*.

•	The opening ceremony was a procession from the Loop to Jackson Park, and at the head of the procession was President Grover Cleveland. Included were 23 carriages, filled with world leaders, monarchs and tycoons, followed on foot, horseback and streetcars by 200,000 Chicagoans.

•	Fairgoers tasted a new snack called Cracker Jack and a new breakfast food called Shredded Wheat. Pancake fixins in a box was introduced under the name of Aunt Jemima's. The Wisconsin Pavilion featured a 22,000 pound wheel of cheese, which somehow did not mold during the 6 months of the Fair.

•	The exposition's top beer award, their Blue Ribbon, was won by a beer that up until the time of the Fair was known as Pabst. Immediately after the Fair, the beer name was officially changed to Pabst Blue Ribbon Beer.

•	The Fair was so big that it required its own police force, fire department, hospital, ambulance service, water-sterilization plant, rail system, and so many horses that tons of manure had to be handled each day.

•	Olmstead's men created a central lagoon, around which all of the Fair's main buildings would rise. In the lagoon's middle was a gorgeous Wooded Island. People were transported from building to building on small electric boats through lagoon waters teeming with ducks, pelicans, pigeons, storks, egrets, flamingoes, and geese. Below the formal terraces of the buildings, Olmstead positioned fragrant plants to further enhance the experience.

•	The Fair helped change the history of electricity by installing the newly patented alternating currents of a Mister George Westinghouse to illuminate the exposition, rather than the established direct current electricity offered by General Electric. This was the biggest demonstration of electric illumination anywhere, ever, and the first large-scale use of alternating current. Every building was outlined in white light bulbs and the giant search lights mounted on the tallest building were visible 60 miles away. During its 6 month run, the Fair used 3 times the electricity than that used by the entire city.

•	For the vast majority of Fair visitors, it was their first exposure ever to electric street lights. Live music from an orchestra in New York could be heard through a long-distance telephone. People saw the first moving pictures from Thomas Alva Edison's Kinetoscope. The first all-electric kitchen was displayed, complete with a dishwasher.

•	The Children's Building had a daycare for the kids, and when you dropped them off you received in return a claim check. Out of the hundreds of thousands of children left at the daycare, only one child was not picked up by his parents.

•	Within the Fair's 4,000+ work force was Elias Disney, who greatly influenced his son Walt's career path through his many stories about the wonders of the Fair.

•	Fair attendees included Teddy Roosevelt, Houdini, Edison, Joplin, Darrow, Woodrow Wilson, the brilliant Polish Pianist Paderewski, Helen Keller, Diamond Jim Brady, Frank Lloyd Wright, Annie Oakley & Buffalo Bill Cody (who drew 4 million to his Buffalo Bill's Wild West Show, adjacent to the Fairgrounds).

•	Since 1893, inspired by the Fair, every carnival has a Ferris Wheel & a Midway.

It was noted that the Fair seemed to put people in awe, as if they were in the presence of something far greater than the beauty of the surroundings, and as a result people spoke softly, moved gently, and seemed to be under a wonderful spell. Some people were seen weeping upon viewing the structures in the Court of Honor. It was, said Edgar Masters, "an inexhaustible dream of beauty". Visitors said that no amount of newspaper articles or word of mouth could prepare them for what they saw. When the Fair closed, many came to the fairgrounds for one last visit, as if paying their respects to passing loved one. Many Fair structures were destroyed in an 1894 fire which, strangely, brought relief for many who did not want the Fair's grandeur to slowly rot away. One building had a brick substructure and survived the fire, the Palace of Fine Arts. Today, you can see this same building overlooking Olmstead's lagoon and referred to by its current name, the Museum of Science and Industry, in the Hyde Park neighborhood along Lake Michigan.

The Director of the 1893 Great Chicago World's Fair was architect Daniel Burnham. His experience at the Fair showed him, and all the fairgoers, how great a city could be. Clean drinking water, clean public restrooms, the safety of electric streetlights, an ambulance service, and children's daycare were all novelties of the times – until the Fair. Civic leaders in the USA and beyond asked Burnham to adapt the Fair's model for their city. Each time refusing a fee, he designed citywide plans for San Francisco, Manila, and Cleveland. In Washington D.C., the green that extends from the Capitol to the Lincoln Memorial is due to Burnham persuading the head of the Pennsylvania Railroad to remove the railroad's depot and freight tracks from the center of the federal mall.

Daniel Burnham's final urban plan was for his hometown, Chicago. Only a portion of his *1909 Plan of Chicago* (also known as "the Burnham Plan") became a reality, resulting in Chicago's system of lakefront parks (reserving 25 of the city's 29 lakefront miles for the public) and Michigan Avenue's "Magnificent Mile". Burnham Park, named in his honor, is located along the section of the lakefront that includes Soldier Field, McCormick Place and the Field Museum, which he designed, all the way south to the Museum of Science and Industry.

Camping near Chicago? Within 90 minutes of the city are the twelve campgrounds listed below. For further information check www.dnr.illinois.gov

1. Kankakee River State Park, 5314 W. Rt. 102 in Bourbonnais IL 60914; (815) 933-1383
2. Channahon State Park, 2 West Story Rd in Channahon IL 60410; (815) 467-4271
3. Burnidge & Paul Wolff Forest Preserves on Coombs Road (west of Randall Road) in Kane County IL; (847) 741-9924
4. Gebhard Woods on 401 Ottawa St. in Morris IL 60450; (815) 942-0796
5. Buffalo Rock State Park at 1300 North 27th Rd. in Ottawa IL 61350; (815) 433-2220
6. Glacial Park, 6316 Harts Rd, Ringwood IL 60072; (815) 338-6223
7. Shabbona Lake State Park, 100 Preserve Rd, Shabbona IL 60550; (815) 824-2106
8. Chain O'Lakes State Park, 8916 Wilmot Rd., Spring Grove IL 60081; (847) 587-5512
9. Blackwell Forest Preserve, Butterfield Rd & Rte. 59, Warrenville IL 60555; (630) 933-7200
10. Pratt's Wayne Woods, Powis Road N of Army Trail Rd, Wayne IL; (630) 933-7248
11. Des Plaines State Fish & Wildlife Area, 24621 N. River Rd., Wilmington IL 60481; (815) 423-5326
12. Illinois Beach State Park, Wadsworth Rd., Zion IL 60099; (847) 662-4811

THE TAVERNS: GREEN DOOR TAVERN & (R.I.P.) MCCUDDY'S

Green Door Tavern, 678 N. Orleans St., Chicago; (312) 664-5496

Within the first year of Mrs. O'Leary's Cow starting the Great Chicago Fire of 1871, a man named James McCole built the structure that today houses the Green Door Tavern. McCole completed his work just before the city passed a 1872 fire code ordinance that prohibited new construction of wooden commercial buildings. As a result of that timing, the Green Door Tavern is one of Chicago's few remaining wooden structures.

The tavern seems to be listing a bit. No, it's not because you've knocked down a few too many and no, you do not need to chug your beer and head quickly for the exits: the bar's exterior lean has been that way since the 1870s, shortly after the building settled.

You have to figure that the authorities really weren't trying all that hard: the origin of the name "Green Door Tavern" is from Prohibition days. Back then, if a restaurant door was painted green, there was a speakeasy (i.e. a blind pig) selling alcohol illegally within.

Today, the door is still green where it says, "Established 1921, famous for our home-style cooking", which includes on the menu the "legendary Green Door Burger" (it _was_ very good!). If you like old time taverns at all, you'll love this place as soon as you walk in.

As cool as the main floor is, and it is, if at all possible check out the downstairs. You feel as if you've walked into the Roaring 20s. Used primarily for private parties, this floor was where the tavern's speakeasy was located. The back bar is a 20' long gorgeous oak piece with some sweet looking metal inlays. Above the back bar hangs a 48 star Old Glory. The National Cash Register Co. of Dayton, Ohio provides another fine Prohibition era piece. Keeping with the day's paddling theme is a classic Hamm's Beer sign that includes a beached canoe, a nearby tent and a waterfall in the background. It's all so fine, but maybe the most fascinating part of the old speakeasy is what lies behind the curtain, and the curtain itself…

The ancient red stage curtain reads across the top, "Japanese Wonder / born on the Pacific Ocean/ adults only" while the draped left side says "Part a Boy" and the draped right "Part a Girl". Behind the curtain is what may be possibly the world's oldest surviving pinball machine. It's "ten plays for 5 cents" and there's no glitzy machine graphics to dazzle and draw you in. No sir, just cornstalks drawn on the playing surface. Back in the day, your ability to influence the pinball action was limited as this machine has no flippers.

Upstairs or downstairs, you will love this bar!

MCCUDDY'S TAVERN

McCuddy's Tavern, 35th and Shields, Chicago; the number's been disconnected (to quote the B52s)

Born February 1910, died March 1988. Lived one helluva full and fun life. The building may crumble, but not the memories. During Babe Ruth's 1914-1935 major league career, whenever his team was in town, you were likely to see him at McCuddy's. The tavern was directly across the street from old Comiskey Park, allowing the Babe plenty of time between games of a doubleheader to, while still in his uniform, visit Ma McCuddy who would set Ruth up with a beer or two and a roast beef sandwich or two ("He ate everything he could eat & drink in 3 minutes" according to Ma's granddaughter). Babe gave Ma an oversized baseball bat that she hung on the wall behind the bar. It was my good fortune (thanks Pete Armstrong) to make my single McCuddy's visit just before they closed. That bat was still on the wall in 1988 and the Babe's inscription on the bat read, *To "Ma" McCuddy from Babe Ruth 1927*. When he played at Comiskey, Ruth would send messages to McCuddy's late in the game such as "Ma, put six bottles of beer on ice – it's two out in the ninth." Many of Ruth's visits occurred during Prohibition, but it's believed that didn't prevent him from getting a beer (and not near beer, either). Babe had a special relationship with Ma, calling her the best woman in the world, and she evidently felt highly of Ruth in return, since he was the only ballplayer allowed to wear spikes into McCuddy's.

Ma McCuddy cooked for the old time ballplayers and she was "Ma" to them all. They'd be at the tavern before, after and sometimes, like the Babe, between games. What that must have been like, to be a baseball fan drinking a beer in the midst of a tavern full of baseball players from the great eras of the teens, 20s, 30s, etc.

One of the most fascinating and funny individuals in the annals of baseball was former White Sox owner & Chicago native Bill Veeck. Veeck spent many hours in McCuddy's, drinking beer and talking baseball with the fans. Who wouldn't have loved talking baseball with the man who once said (this coming from a baseball owner, mind you), "I have discovered in 20 years of moving around a ballpark, that the knowledge of the game is usually in inverse proportion to the price of the seats."

Among McCuddy's other regulars were George Wendt (aka Norm Peterson; "Can I draw you a beer Norm?" "No, I know what they look like, just pour me one") and Chicago Bears defensive lineman Dan Hampton.

McCuddy's opened 5 months before play began at the original Comiskey Park in July 1910. Construction of the new Comiskey, scheduled to open in 1991, was to begin in 1989 and since McCuddy's stood where the 3rd base line of the new park runs, the old building had to go. Good intentions and promises from city officials to move McCuddy's to a new site did not materialize. After 78 years, McCuddy's Tavern would be no more.

For those of you who love old time taverns where friends meet to drink beer and talk baseball, you'll love this interview with Frances McCuddy (begins 47 seconds in)… http://www.youtube.com/watch?v=NI4fb_O7Zeo. You will also have newfound respect for 1980s White Sox Julio Cruz and Tom Paciorek (as a Detroit native who grew up in Hamtramck, Tom knew a good bar when he saw one).

35th and Shields – what a great place to have been!

Sources: www.chicagohs.org, The Devil In The White City by Erik Larson, Encyclopedia of Chicago, Wikipedia, the Green Door Tavern, Chicago Bars of the Past video by Tom Weinberg, My Baseball Diary by James Farrell, www.chicagoreader.com, www.kendall.edu, Kayak Chicago, Don Rogers, www.chicagoarchitecture.info

CHIPPEWA RIVER

CHIPPEWA FALLS, WI
TRIP 3.5 MILES & 1 HOURS 33 MINUTES LONG

BEGINNER ABILITY

LIVERY: LOOPY'S RENTALS SALOON & GRILL, 10691 BUSINESS HIGHWAY 29 (1 MILE WEST OF TOWN), CHIPPEWA FALLS WI 54729, (715) 723-5667, www.723loop.com. OWNERS LORI AND BILL "LOOPY" KLEICH.

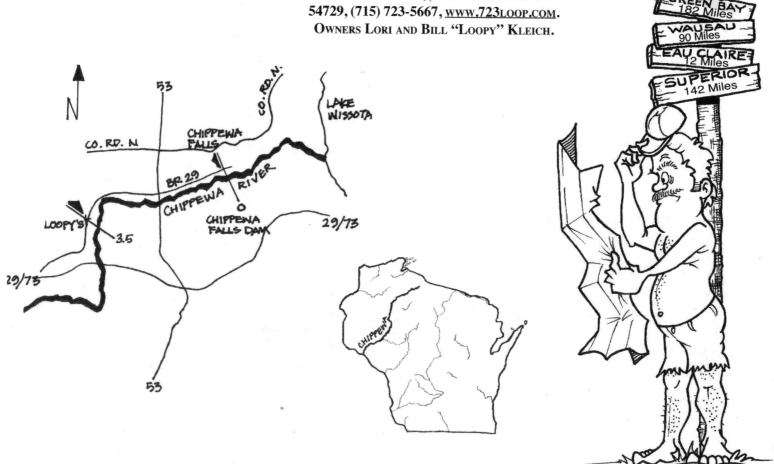

CHIPPEWA RIVER

SOUNDTRACK: MONDO CARAVAN – THE CARAVANS, DINER
– MARTIN SEXTON, ALWAYS LOOK ON THE BRIGHT SIDE
OF LIFE – MONTY PYTHON, EARLY IN THE MORNING
– LOUIS JORDAN, PETER GUNN – HENRY MANCINI

RIVER QUOTE...
OVERHEARD: "THE POLICE NEVER THINK
IT'S AS FUNNY AS YOU DO"

The Chippewa River has its headwaters in the northwest section of Wisconsin, and from there it flows for 180 miles in a south & southwesterly direction until it empties into the Mississippi River. The Chippewa run begins with its twin forks: the East Fork begins 20 miles straight south of the western most end of Michigan's Upper Peninsula (so 20 miles south of Lake Superior), while the West Fork begins in the SE corner of Bayfield County near Clam Lake. The two forks of the Chippewa merge together at the Lake Chippewa Flowage, 15 miles east of Hayward.

The Lake Chippewa Flowage was created in 1924 by the building of a dam across the Chippewa River. The dam joined together the water from 9 rivers and 11 lakes, resulting in 200 miles of shoreline and 15,000 acres of water, home to over 140 islands. Excellent canoeing & kayaking fun awaits you throughout the Flowage.

From the merger of the East and West Forks, the Chippewa River heads to a rendezvous with the Mississippi River, 50 miles to the southwest of Eau Claire. Along the way, the tributaries flowing into the Chippewa River include the Flambeau, Jump, Yellow, Eau Claire and Red Cedar rivers.

The stretch of the Chippewa River outlined in this chapter takes you through the town of Chippewa Falls. Except for a brief rapids run 2/10ths of a mile into the float, the current is mild and well-suited to beginners. The launch site is the Chippewa Falls Hydroelectric Dam, built in 1928, and once the location of one of the largest sawmills in the world.

A state-record, over 26" long, smallmouth bass was caught in the Chippewa River (25" was the record), but was eaten by a hungry fisherman before the catch could be registered. Or so the story goes. Musky and sturgeon are also found in the river.

Loopin' down the Chippewa was Kenny Umphrey, Busch & Julie Beyer, Pete & Peggy Armstrong, & Doc. Our paddling adventure was in June.

THE RIVER: PADDLING THE CHIPPEWA

Launch a few feet downstream from the Chippewa Falls Hydroelectric Dam, from a site where the Falls used to run. The dam is at the Bridge Street / Business Route 29 Bridge.

The trip ends when you take out at Loopy's on the right shore.

The Chippewa River depth is 3' at the put in point. The depth on today's trip will vary from shallow enough to scrape the river's floor to a maximum depth of 15' to 20'. The river width fluctuates from 150' to 200'.

.2 mi/4 min: there's a short rapids run over many rocks lying just below the water's surface. These rapids may be non-existent in deeper (normal) water depth. You're about to float under the Main Street Bridge.

.6 mi/11 min: paddle beneath the Wisconsin Central Line Bridge. Merganser ducks are viewed along the south shore.

1 mi/21 min: reach two midstream islands, each with a rocky base. This is a very straight river – you can turnaround and see one mile back to the dam near our launch site, and then look forward and see the Highway 53 Bridge ahead at the 2 mile mark.

1.5 mi/38 min: when you see the "Pactiv" building beyond the right shore, you'll know that you're one & one-half miles into the trip. The current has slowed gradually since the launch.

1.8 mi/48 min: three small islands lie left of midstream with pilings among them. Beyond the islands and to the left is a footbridge spanning a merging creek.

2 mi/54 min: paddle beneath the Highway 53 Bridge.

2.5 mi/1 hr 7 min: there's a noticeable up tick in the river speed; the GPS tells us it has increased from 2 mph to 4 mph.

2.7 mi/1 hr 10 min: a slow-moving creek merges from the left. Downstream from the creek, there's a fine rock outcropping on the left bank.

2.8 mi/1 hr 13 min: looks like a party island right of midstream. Bottom skimming ensues.

3.1 mi/1 hr 20 min: a creek merging from the right is fronted by a stone island.

3.5 miles/1 hour 33 minutes: you're in! Loopy's is just beyond the right shore.

THE TOWN: CHIPPEWA FALLS

Green Bay Packer local radio station affiliate: WATQ-FM 106.7
Milwaukee Brewer local radio station affiliate: WATQ-FM 106.7/WBIZ-AM 1400

Chippewa Falls lies on that crazy latitude upon where both the Green Bay Packers and the Minnesota Vikings play. The town is located in west-central Wisconsin, 3 hours west of Green Bay and an hour and 45 minutes east of Minneapolis.

Chippewa Falls status as fun to visit is reflected in the honors it's received. It was listed as one of America's Top Ten Small Towns by *Time Magazine,* its Main Street once won the "Great American Main Street Award", and the town was designated as "One of a Dozen Distinctive Destinations" by the *National Trust For Historic Preservation* folks.

Many fascinating personalities, human & otherwise, left their mark on the area's history:

Old Abe the War Eagle On Highway 178 in Jim Falls, just NE of Chippewa Falls, is a statue honoring Old Abe the War Eagle. In 1861, hungry Native Americans from the Chippewa tribe came to the local McCann farm looking for food. The family traded corn to the Chippewa in exchange for the tribe's young eagle. When the Eighth Wisconsin was organized for duty in the Civil War, the McCann Family offered the eagle to act as the troop's mascot. During 42 battles, Old Abe would fly above and scream encouragement to the men. The louder the noise in battle, the louder and fiercer Old Abe would scream.

After Old Abe's war service ended in 1864, he was formally presented to the State of Wisconsin. A room at the State Capitol was prepared for him and a caretaker hired for Abe. At the 1880 Milwaukee *National Encampment of the Grand Army of the Republic*, Old Abe was honored (a fella by the name of U.S. Grant was honored that day, too).

Jean Brunet was born in France and moved to Chippewa Falls in 1828. This Renaissance man built the areas first dams on the Chippewa River, was the town's first judge and first member of the legislature for the County. Brunet piloted the first raft of lumber to travel the river from the Falls to the Mississippi River, floating the raft down the Mississippi south to Prairie DuChien. Brunet also piloted the first steamboat up the Chippewa River. He was loved and respected by both the Native Americans and the White settlers.

Seymour Cray was born in Chippewa Falls in 1925. In 1960, he designed the first computer to be fully transistorized. In 1970, he was credited with creating the world's first super computer. Through his Chippewa Falls-based company, Cray Research, he was directly responsible for the design and development of computer systems that were the fastest in the world for many years. The first Cray-1 system was installed at the Los Alamos National Lab in 1976. Once asked why he often hires new graduates to help him with early R&D work, he replied, "Because they don't know that what I'm asking them to do is impossible, so they try."

Jack Dawson Leonardo DiCaprio's fictional character from the movie *Titanic* was born and lived in Chippewa Falls.

Jacob Leinenkugel opened in 1867, with John Miller, the Spring Brewery Co. In 1883, Jacob bought out his friend and eventually changed the brewery name to the Jacob Leinenkugel Brewing Company. Leinenkugel's, Chippewa Fall's oldest industry, is run by fifth generation family members (a special thanks to the family for Honey Weiss). Any brewery that provides canoe-shaped taps to bars selling their beers is one deserving of a visit. After a free tour of the brewery, cross over Duncan Creek (on a gorgeous foot bridge) to Leinie's Lodge where you can conclude the tour with two free 7 oz. beers.

Nearby camping is available at Lake Wissota State Park, just northeast of town. Among their 1,062 forested acres are 81 campsites, 17 with electricity. The park has 17 miles of hiking trails and a 285 foot swimming beach. The address is 18127 County Hwy O in Chippewa Falls 54729. Call (715) 382-4574.

THE TAVERN: LOOPY'S RENTALS SALOON & GRILL

As a place to kick back after a day on the river, a tavern located along that river has a built-in advantage versus taverns surrounded on all sides by dry land. When you add the fact that this tavern also rents canoes & kayaks to you, drops you off upstream, allowing you to float back to the tavern and your vehicles, well what you got here is the merger of beer, location, and some good thinking. What you got here is a place called Loopy's.

The 3 and one-half mile river trip ends at Loopy's Deck on the riverbank, right below Loopy's backyard. In Loopy's backyard is a Tiki Bar overlooking the river, a 30' by 60' tent, 3 regulation size sand volleyball courts, a bean bag toss area, fire pit, and plenty of picnic tables.

Once inside Loopy's, we were greeted by a lunch buffet (with pizza!) with a side helping of darts, video machines, and a big screen TV. Friday nights at Loopy's feature their "Leinie's Honey Weiss Fish Fry" (oh, that sounds good!). Summertime Friday's kick the fun up a notch with live music.

Among all this goodness, what seemed to really grab our paddling group's attention was Loopy's Bloody Marys. Apparently, they've piqued some other folks' interest, too. We visited during a Monday lunchtime to find the waitress suffering from "Bloody Mary Elbow", a common problem we were told, after making so many over the weekend. Fellow paddler Julie, a Bloody Mary connoisseur, said these are among the best she'd ever had. Each comes with an olive, pepper, pickle, cheese & beef stick (*On Wisconsin!*).

Loopy's is located at 10691 Business Hwy 29, 1 mile west of town, ph (715) 723-5667.

Sources: www.bridgehunter.com, Chippewa Falls Main Street, Inc., Chippewa County Historical Markers, a tribute to Seymour Cray, Chippewa Falls Museum of Industry & Technology, Leinenkugel Brewery Tour, Wikipedia

EAU CLAIRE RIVER

EAU CLAIRE, WI
TRIP 8.2 MILES & 3 HOURS 15 MINUTES LONG

VETERAN ABILITY REQUIRED

Livery: Riverside Junction, mailing address E20355 County Road Nd, Augusta WI 54722. On Hwy 27 at the Eau Claire River, 5 miles north of Augusta; (715) 456-2434, www.riversidejunction.com. Owner Dave Steele.

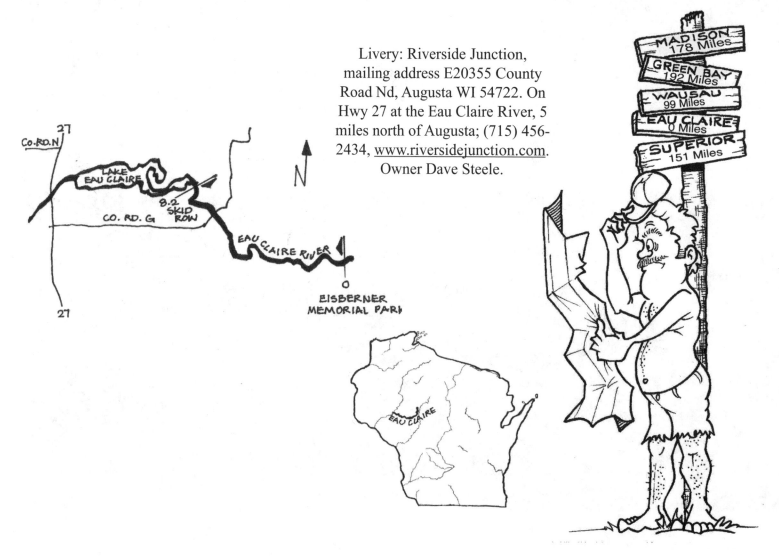

EAU CLAIRE RIVER

SOUNDTRACK: ODYSSEY – THE THUNDERMEN,
BACK IN TOWN – UW-EC JAZZ ENSEMBLE I,
QUIET VILLAGE – DANNY GATTON, WHIPPING POST – ALLMAN
BROTHERS, BRIDGE OVER TROUBLED WATERS – JOHNNY CASH

RIVER QUOTES...
DAVE STEELE: "IT'S MY EXPERIENCE IN THE WILDERNESS THAT THERE'S
NOT A PLACE ON EARTH THAT YOU CAN'T GET A BEER CAN TO"
DOC: "WE WERE SUPPOSED TO SEE SOME PRETTY GOOD ROCK FORMATIONS.
I DIDN'T KNOW THAT THEY'D ALL BE BELOW THE WATER'S SURFACE"

"Pretty wild in May and plenty exciting in June" was how River Junction owner Dave Steele described the Eau Claire River to us. Dave knows his river. Our Eau Claire float took place in June, and the river was a joy to paddle with its uncrowded feel, several exciting rapids, and fabulous wildlife including a deer running up a creek *towards* us with a crane flying right behind and swooping down low as if in pursuit, an eagle flying overhead, merganser ducks, and turtles racing (yes, *racing*) across a wide beach.

Eau Claire is from the French *Eaux Claires* meaning clear waters. Legend has it that early French explorers, after canoeing down the muddier Chippewa River, arrived at this tributary and exclaimed *Voici l'eau claire!* ("Here is clear water!"). From the headwaters of its two forks until it ends at the town of Eau Claire, where it empties into the Chippewa River, the Eau Claire River flows westward for 75 miles.

This is not a trip for beginners: in the stretch of the Eau Claire River outlined in this chapter, the frequent rapids and rocks encountered require experienced paddlers.

The Riverside Junction livery offers 5 trips on the Eau Claire River, one on Lake Eau Claire, and what sounds like a wonderfully isolated trip up the North Fork of the river.

For the fishermen, musky are abundant in the Eau Claire River.

Paddling the Eau Claire in June was Kenny Umphrey, Pete & Peggy Armstrong, & Doc.

THE RIVER: PADDLING THE EAU CLAIRE

Launch at the Donald A. Eisberner Memorial Forest & Canoe Landing, just downstream from the confluence of the North & South Forks of the Eau Claire, on Canoe Landing Forest Road, south of Channey Road & 2.5 miles west of County Road H. The trip ends at the Skid Row Landing, where the Eau Claire River becomes Lake Eau Claire.

At the Eau Claire River launch, the river width is 60', about what it will average for the duration of this stretch. The depth ranges from bottom-scraping to 3'.

3 minutes into the trip, a large and sprawling sandy beach on the left covers 2/3rds of the river. 2 minutes later and on the left sits a stone chimney for a house that once was.

.9 mi/21 min: at the end of a long straightaway that is well-populated with rocks, the river bends left into a 2-minute long run of class 1 rapids.

1.5 mi/43 min: an island right of midstream is passable on either side.

1.8 mi/50 min: *give this approach your full attention!* Through challenging class 2 rapids known as *Coon Fork Rapids*, paddle to the left around an island. Passage to the right is blocked by large rocks.

2 mi/58 min: a very active and large creek merges from the left. At the merger, the sandy beach on the left is guarded by rocks.

2.4 mi/1 hr 6 min: a great break spot is at the nice sandy beach on your left as the river bends left.

2.5 mi/1 hr 10 min: at a big oxbow bend to the left is the beginning of a stretch of 30' tall dunes on the right shore. These are called the *Yellow Banks* and will continue on for the next 6 minutes (3/10ths of a mile long). On the right shore of the river, across from the start of the dunes, is a fine break location.

3 mi/1 hr 20 min: at the upstream end of an island the main body of the Eau Claire flows to the right and through a rock garden. What starts as class 1 rapids becomes class 2s.

3.3 mi/1 hr 28 min: picturesque rock outcroppings lie across the river from a sandy beach on the right bank.

3.5 mi/1 hr 35 min: begin a 3 minute run of riffles and light class 1 rapids.

3.8 mi/1 hr 42 min: a challenging class 1 runs where the river is compressed by a stone buildup extending from the right bank.

4.1 mi/1 hr 50 min: gravel and sand beach, where past campfire use is evident, is on the left as the river bends left. Across the river, pretty little Whippoorwill Creek winds its way to a merger with the river.

4.6 mi/1 hr 58 min: where an island lies right of midstream, a tiny creek merges from the left.

5 mi/2 hrs 7 min: float beneath the Troubled Water Bridge at County Road G. 5 minutes later pass a large sandy beach on the left, across from a creek just downstream, then a larger beach right.

6 mi/2 hrs 30 min: 5' high "baby dunes" are on the right across the river from a rock and sand beach. Upon seeing our boats, two turtles raced (<u>much</u> faster than you could've imagined!) across the 40' to 50' open space on the beach to the river's safety.

6.4 mi/2 hrs 36 min: the first of two consecutive fine break spots, separated by 3 minutes, are on beaches along the left shore.

6.6 mi/2 hrs 44 min: a big logjam along the right shore provides a logging days flashback moment. Just downstream a creek merges from the right.

6.8 mi/2 hrs 46 min: as the river bends right, a large sandy beach beckons on the right as an eagle flies above us.

7 mi/2 hrs 50 min: you'll know that you're at the lucky 7-mile mark when the river comes to a "T". Here, the river flows left while a big creek merges from the right. And lucky it is. There's a wildlife viewing bonanza as a deer races up the creek towards us followed closely by a crane swooping down low as if in pursuit (such an unusual and beautiful scene). Just ahead are merganser ducks.

7.5 mi/3 hrs: at the end of a long straightaway as the river bends left, a creek 10' wide at its mouth merges from the right. 3 minutes later you reach the upstream end of an island, passable on either side. A creek merges on the island's right.

8 mi/3 hrs 8 min: the river widens to a bay; a creek half the width of the river merges from the left.

8.2 miles/3 hours 15 minutes: you're in! The Skid Row access is on the left, and is at the end of the Eau Claire River and at the start of Lake Eau Claire, approximately 5 miles to the east of the Riverside Junction livery. The Skid Row take out is just before the dock and homes, which are also on the left shore. There are restrooms, but no camping, at this access. Dave Steele wants you to know that there is a $3 access fee at Skid Row, with a $185 fine if you don't pay – and the authorities enforce it!

THE TOWN: EAU CLAIRE

Green Bay Packer local radio station affiliate: WATQ-FM 106.7
Milwaukee Brewer local radio station affiliate: WATQ-FM 106.7/WBIZ-AM 1400

The town of Eau Claire has been referred to as "unexpected Wisconsin". Bob Seger said that he wrote the song "Turn the Page" in an Eau Claire hotel room. That IS unexpected!

Eau Claire's 65,000 residents live in a community consistently ranked as one of the USA's safest. It is located 90 miles to the east of Minneapolis and along the northern edge of the "driftless region", the section of Wisconsin bypassed by glaciers during the Ice Age. Since the area was untouched by glaciers, the glaciers heavy sediment known as drift did not flatten or erode the local rock outcroppings, leaving for us the beautiful rock formations that we see today (such as those southeast of town at the Lake Eau Claire County Park – see below).

The town has a certain cool about it in its design, its stores, outdoor festivals (downtown and beyond), and how it interacts with the waterfront. That waterfront is created by the merger of the Eau Claire River and the Chippewa River, which takes place in the heart of downtown (one of the great views of this river merger is from 1st Avenue).

Eau Claire's position along the confluence of the two rivers made it the perfect location for logging interests, and as many as 22 area sawmills operated on the rivers in the 1800s. A few minutes east of the Eau Claire and Chippewa Rivers merger is the Randall Park Historic District where 19th century lumber barons built their homes a comfortable carriage ride from their business operations. Take the time to visit the beautiful Randall Park community and its 25 buildings found on the National Register of Historic Places.

Eau Claire's Third Ward has as a resident the University of Wisconsin – Eau Claire. The campus, located on the banks

of the Chippewa River with its great bike trails and tucked into the gorgeous north woods, is often described as Wisconsin's most beautiful campus.

The university's *Jazz Studies Area* has received Down Beat Magazine's "Best College Big Band" award 6 times. Two CDs released by the school's "Jazz Ensemble I" have received Grammy award nominations, and the band's

1991 China performance was the first by a western jazz band since before the days of Mao Tse-tung. The university is heavily involved with the Eau Claire Jazz Festival, which began in 1968 and is one of the USA's longest running jazz festivals.

In the city's center is an island called Carson Park. On the island is a baseball park of the same name. Carson Park is a very intimate, old time park, with wooden seats so close to the field that you feel a part of the action. This is a park that gives hardcore baseball fans goose bumps. The park opened for play in 1937, and was one of FDR's Works Progress Administration (WPA) projects. Over the years, ballplayers from the Eau Claire Bears/ Braves included Billy Bruton, Andy Pafko, Wes Covington, Joe Torre, Bob Uecker, and the man who broke Babe Ruth's all-time home run record, Hank Aaron (together with his brother Tommie, Hank also holds the all-time record for home runs by brothers with 768: Hank's 755 and Tommie's 13). On June 14, 1952, the 18-year old Henry Aaron made his pro baseball debut at Carson Park, hitting run-scoring singles in his first two at bats. Aaron's 1952 .336 batting average and stalwart defensive play earned him a spot on the Northern League All-Star team as well as the league's Rookie of the Year award. By 1954, Hammerin' Hank was promoted to the major leagues with the Milwaukee Braves, retiring in 1976 while playing with the Milwaukee Brewers. On 8.17.94, in front of Carson Park and with Aaron in attendance, a statue was unveiled that depicts Hank as that 18-year old Eau Claire Braves shortstop from 1952.

A beautiful and historic setting is found southeast of Eau Claire and is 1/10th of a mile east of the Riverside Junction livery, a place called Lake Eau Claire County Park. There is no camping at this park, which is located on County S-D Road, just east of Highway 27 and on the south shore of Lake Eau Claire. The park is a 1930's WPA project and the park's clubhouse is the old WPA mess hall, measuring 40' x 100' with a large fireplace. Along with the clubhouse, you may reserve one of the park's six picnic shelters and its bbq pit shelter. The park includes a baseball diamond, horseshoe pits, a playground and two volleyball courts. You can fish off one of the two park mooring docks on Lake Eau Claire. Across the lake from the park are wonderful rock outcroppings. Ph 715-286-2681.

Area camping includes the Coon Fork Lake County Park, about two miles south of the river's Eisberner launch site, on Goat Ranch Road near County Hwy CF. Ph 715-839-4783; right along the Eau Claire River and one-half hour downstream from Riverside Junction are the Harstad County Park campgrounds. Ph 715-286-5536.

THE TAVERN: BLACK BEAR SUPPER CLUB

The Black Bear Supper Club is directly across the Eau Claire River from the Riverside Junction canoe/kayak livery, the Black Bear on the north side and the livery on the south.

Our Eau Claire River crack research team loves the Black Bear ribs: "These ribs are better than any in Chicago, and I don't have bad meals in Chicago" said Peggy; "The ribs are phenomenal… meaty & tasty!" said Kenny. It seems that the ribs are a part of the reason that the Black Bear was voted one of Wisconsin's top 10 supper clubs by both *Milwaukee Journal Sentinel* and the *Wisconsin State Journal*.

As soon as you enter, you're struck by the beautiful dark pine walls. The U-shaped bar lends itself to interacting with your friends. This bar was built in 1930 from the ground up by its first owners, a husband and wife team. The 110-year old tin roof (with great detail) was brought over from an old school house for the 1930 construction. The current building is in its original state except for some added backroom facilities. The life-sized stuffed bears inside were added in 1955. The front cover of the menu pictures a black bear sitting at a picnic table, looking like he's waiting to be fed.

Current owners Jean and Keith had an interesting welcome to bar ownership: visiting their newly purchased establishment, a black bear was sitting under the "Black Bear

Supper Club" sign. They thought it was a neat statue – until it moved. The husband and wife owners make for an entertaining ying and yang, the city fella and the country gal, Keith the excellent cook and Jean the personable conversationalist…

"Jean, may we buy you a drink?"
"No, I just drink at will around here"

"Jean, what's the biggest surprise about owning a bar?"
"How much the government gets"

When told about the subject of this book, Jean suggested that we entitle it, "Canoeing Rivers in the State of Mosquitoes and Beer".

    The Christmas tree stays up all year, decorated by Jean to reflect the changing seasons: Packer football, Valentines, Easter, fishing, etc.

    Great food, beautiful interior, classic old structure, and fun owners make the Black Bear Supper Club a wonderful place to visit after a day on the Eau Claire River.

    The Black Bear Supper Club is located at S5450 Highway 27, 5 miles north of Augusta, on the north bank of the Eau Claire River, ph (715) 286-2687.

Sources: Dave Steele, state historical markers, www.genesis10.com, Wikipedia, University of Wisconsin – Eau Claire, Carson Park statues, Shriner Dick Mitchell, Black Bear owners Jean & Keith

FLAMBEAU RIVER SOUTH FORK

PHILLIPS, WI
TRIP 5.4 MILES & 2 HOURS 4 MINUTES LONG

INTERMEDIATE ABILITY

LIVERY: FLAMBEAU SPORTS OUTFITTERS CANOE OUTFITTING & GUIDE SERVICE, N11151 COUNTY ROAD F, PHILLIPS WI 54555, (715) 339-2012, WWW.FLAMBEAUSPORTS.COM. OWNER DAVID KELLY (DAVE'S LIVERY AND GENERAL STORE ARE IN DOWNTOWN LUGERVILLE).

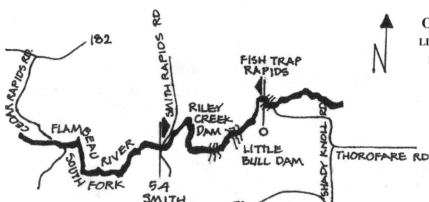

FLAMBEAU RIVER SOUTH FORK

Early 1600s French explorers came upon Native Americans fishing the river at night from their canoes, using flaming torches to light the way. In French, "flambeau" means "flaming torch".

The South Fork of the Flambeau runs west/southwest for 68 miles through the center of northern Wisconsin. Its headwaters run downhill from Round Lake in Northeast Price County, about 50 miles south of Lake Superior. The South Fork merges into the bigger North Fork (a 120 mile long river) in the Flambeau River State Forest at a place called "The Forks", about 10 miles north of the town of Ingram.

The section of the South Fork detailed in this chapter begins 2 miles downstream from its Round Lake headwaters, under the Forest Road 144 Bridge, at a place called Fish Trap Rapids. To access the Forest Road 144 Bridge, take Highway 70 for 16.5 miles east of Fifield to Shady Knoll Road and drive north for 4 miles to the bridge. From here, the river runs southwest, parallel to and north of the old Fifield Trail (1879 to 1914). You will end your trip about 100 yards beyond the Smith Rapids Covered Bridge. The Smith Rapids bridge is 2 miles north of Highway 70 on Forest Road 148.

This section of the river has long stretches of quiet water. It earns its "Intermediate" degree of difficulty ranking from the 4 short and challenging rapids encountered (not including the beginner-friendly *Little Bull Rapids*).

The Flambeau South Fork has a reputation as an excellent river for smallmouth bass, musky, and walleye fishing.

Paddling the South Fork were the canoe team of Maggie and Doc. The trip was taken in the September.

THE RIVER: THE FLAMBEAU SOUTH FORK

Launch about 10' downstream (west) from the Forest Road 144 Bridge. There is a path leading to the river on the north end of the bridge. The trip ends 2 hours later, 100 yards past the Smith Rapids Covered bridge and on the left bank (look for the gently sloping dirt path).

Upon launching, the river is 2' deep and 15' wide. You're immediately into class 2 rapids known as Fish Trap Rapids. From the bridge, the rapids run for one-fifth of a mile and 5 minutes (the rapids actually begin on the upstream side of the bridge). The rapids end after the 2nd of back-to-back islands. After Fish Trap Rapids, the river averages a width of 30' to 40' and a depth of 2' to 3'.

.4 mi/20 min: see the first in a series of homes on the left shore. The last home in this grouping is at the 1 mile mark. It's a marshy landscape on the right. The river is very dark and, although it's only 2' to 3' deep, you cannot see the bottom.

.8 mi/18 min: on your left are several sets of stairs leading down to the river. On the right are big lily pads.

1 mi/22 min: you'll know that you're 1 mile into the trip when you pass a home sitting on a peninsula, jutting out into the South Fork from the left. Stairs lead from the home to a dock and the river. Soon, the river turns marshy on both your left and your right. Maggie says that you'll notice the "beckoning reeds" just below the surface.

1.4 mi/31 min: a large rock is midstream. It is 4' long, 2' wide, and 1.5' above the surface during our late-summer journey.

1.7 mi/39 min: WHEE! It's a fun 2 & 1/2 foot drop at the *Little Bull Dam Rapids*. These class 2 rapids get you flying through at over 7 miles per hour. Part of the excitement is that you will hear 'em well before you see 'em. As you approach the drop at the old dam site, stay to the right for the safest passage.

1.8 mi/41 min: at the downstream end of an island, enter into a light and short class 1 rapids run known as the *Little Bull Rapids*.

2.1 mi/48 min: once again, you hear 'em before you see 'em. You're at the *Riley Creek Dam Rapids*, a brief class 2 run featuring a 1 & 1/2 foot drop at the old dam site. On this approach to the drop you again stay to the right for safe passage.

Outside of the echoing rapids, the Flambeau trip is a float through a peacefully quiet wilderness. That peacefulness allows you to continue to hear the crashing water of the Riley Creek Dam Rapids, 7 minutes after passing through them.

3.1 mi/1 hr 11 min: a "permanent" strainer may be passed on a 7' opening along both river banks.

3.3 mi/1 hr 18 min: near the right shore are the first of today's pilings sightings. On and off over the next 1.5 miles and 33 minutes is a long run of pilings, both at the river's edge and 5' into the marsh, along each shore. In the woods, you begin to see a great number of birch trees mixed with the pines.

3.8 mi/1 hr 32 min: paddle by 3 consecutive fallen trees from the left bank. Each allows a 5' gap along the right to pass. Two creeks merge from the right.

4.1 mi/1 hr 39 min: float around an oxbow bending left; at its end look downstream to view a beautiful stand of pine packed tightly together, each tree 40' to 50 ' tall. As you paddle closer, note the erosion-fighting stones laid at the base of those pines on the left shore. A similar grouping of stones is seen 10 minutes downstream.

4.7 mi/1 hr 51 min: pass by the last of the pilings, wrapped around the left end of a long straightaway.

5.1 mi/2 hrs: the "Mother Rock", 6' in diameter, is along the left bank on a right bend.

5.2 mi/2 hrs 1 min: look up over the trees and glimpse the top of the Smith Rapids Covered Bridge, waiting around the next bend. This beautiful bridge was built in 1991, but it has the feel of a time 100 years earlier. In seconds you begin to paddle through Smith Rapids. These fun class ones will take you to the trip's end.

5.4 miles/2 hours 4 minutes: you're in! After floating beneath the Smith Rapids Covered Bridge, paddle another 100 yards to the dirt slope on the left bank. You're on the grounds of the Smith Rapids Campgrounds. For information on this fine camp spot, read below "The Town". The rapids continue beyond the dirt slope for as far as the eye can see.

THE TOWN: LUGERVILLE

Green Bay Packer local radio station affiliate: WCQM-FM 98.3
Milwaukee Brewer local radio station affiliate: WCQM-FM 98.3

The South Fork of the Flambeau River runs through the tiny town of Lugerville. Until the early-1900s, Lugerville had more board feet of white pine than anywhere in the USA. In 1904 the Luger Family acquired a large tract of this white pine along the Flambeau. A spur rail line was laid to service this site, and the Lugers constructed the first sawmill in the area. The family built a larger mill in 1905, which was immediately running at full capacity. Homes were built to house all of the newly needed workers and their families, and the town of Lugerville was established. One of those workers was a logger named Ab Smith. The Smith Rapids at the end of this chapter's trip were named after him.

The Luger's sawmill cut enough white pine to supply several furniture manufacturers in the Upper Midwest. So much so, that the white pine was gone by 1909. The Lugers then sold their Lugerville area land to a business that would eventually become the West Lumber Co. This new mill went to work cutting down the area hardwoods, expanding the town's lumber business beyond even the big numbers posted under the Luger family. Lugerville grew to 1,000 residents that were kept fully-employed.

The logging business slowed down as time went on, with the last tree cut by the West Lumber Co. in 1933. Within 3 years, the mill and the company buildings were torn down and the rail lines removed. The town residents soon followed. Today, 30 folks live in Lugerville. The largest building in this small town serves as the office for David Kelly's livery, Flambeau Sports Outfitters Canoe Outfitting & Guide Service.

14 driving miles northeast of Lugerville is another town that sits on the banks of the Flambeau's South Fork, a place originally known as Flambeau. In 1879 that name was changed to Fifield (named after a timber magnate of the day), which is located at the junction of Highways 70 & 13. On the National Register of Historic Places is Fifield's Old Town Hall Museum. Built in 1894, the structure served as a government building until 1967. Today the museum makes an excellent place to visit for those interested in viewing logging artifacts circa 1870s to 1930s. Their gift shop sells books on northern Wisconsin history, from the logging era and beyond.

Lugerville and Fifield are both communities in Price County, a recreational paradise. Within Price County are 150,000 acres of the Chequamegon-Nicolet National Forest, 30,000 acres of state forest land & 92,000 acres of county forest land. Through the county runs hundreds of miles of trails for hiking, biking, cross-country skiing, horseback riding & ATV riding. Price County also offers plenty of opportunities for canoeing, boating, & fishing with its 3 rivers, 45 streams, 98 lakes & 6 county parks. Call 1-800-269-4505 or check www.pricecountywi.net.

For camping near the South Fork of the Flambeau, you can't get any more convenient than this: an excellent area campsite is the one that you've floated into at the end of this chapter's South Fork adventure, the Smith Rapids Campground.

The SRC has 11 sites available. To underscore the great deal of horseback riding opportunities in the area (there are 70 miles of trails nearby), 9 of the campsites have hitching posts and are designed to accommodate horse trailers. The SRC sites have fire grills and picnic tables, and the campground has vault toilets and a picnic shelter. From Fifield, travel 12.5 miles east on Highway 70 and turn left (north) on to Forest Road 148 for 2 miles. The entrance to the campgrounds is on a left turn just before the covered bridge. Call (715) 362-1300.

THE TAVERN: RIVERSIDE

Now *this* is a nice place to relax after a great day on the South Fork, and it's hard to miss. The Riverside Bar is 17 miles east of Highway 13 and on the south side of Highway 70; it's 3/4s of a mile east of Shady Knoll Rd/Forest Rd 144 (where you turned for Fish Trap Rapids); it's right next to the waterfall on Foulds Creek; it's across the highway from Pike Lake; and Riverside's parking lot features a very large Pabst Blue Ribbon sign (always a sure sign of quality).

Molly and Les Nordrum have owned the bar since 2008. Molly says, "it feels like it's been since the 1800s",

appropriate since the building housing the Riverside was built by William Foulds in 1883. The Riverside's interior is a comfortable 30' x 30' of fine pine.

The hard work that Molly & Les put into the Riverside make it a very enjoyable place to spend some time at for the tavern's customers. It starts by making local residents and folks who come from far away feel very welcome. Then there was the food, getting big thumbs up from our table for the delicious fried cauliflower and bar burgers. And then there's the little niceties that make the Riverside unique…

* Behind the bar, the backside of a deer stuck out of the wall, as if it had raced across the bar floor and only partially succeeded in leaving. Interestingly, there was a bottle opener positioned in the (hopefully dead) deer's derriere. Perhaps a bit disturbingly, there was a certain joy in having your longneck opened there.

* An old beehive hangs above the bar. A sign taped to the hive's opening reads, "Please register complaints here". A second beehive by the Ladies Room has a sign which reads, "For faster service, insert finger here". Molly & Les did not say if the hives are inactive.

* And then there was the "Shot Master". The Shot Master is a canoe paddle converted to be used on dry land to get wet. Four small coolies are glued or otherwise secured to the paddle, each spaced about a foot apart. While the paddle is placed flat on the bar, a shot glass is placed in each coolie. All shot glasses are filled with drinks chosen by four Shot Master participants. The four stand in front of the paddle, lift it up to their faces, and turn the paddle to down the shots. The Shot Master is guaranteed to warm your innards!

Stop in and say hi to Molly & Les. You'll be glad that you did.

Riverside is located at W727 State Highway 70 in Fifield, phone (715) 762-2211.

Sources: David Kelly, Molly Nordrum, the Luger Furniture Co., www.parkfalls.com, Town of Fifield, www.pricecountry.net, Paddle the Flambeau River – a river guide

GRANT RIVER

BEETOWN, WI
TRIP 5.6 MILES & 2 HOURS 19 MINUTES LONG

BEGINNER ABILITY

LIVERY: GRANT RIVER CANOE &
KAYAK RENTAL (BY RESERVATION ONLY),
7961 COUNTY U WEST, BEETOWN
WI 53802; (608) 794-2342.

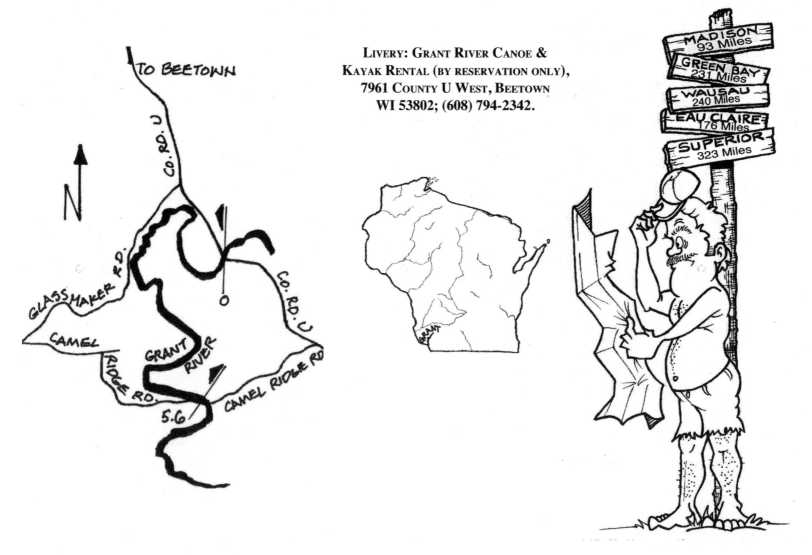

GRANT RIVER

SOUNDTRACK: SIDE-WINDER – THE VIBRATONES,
BUMBLE BEE – B. BUMBLE & THE STINGERS,
TAXI – BOB JAMES, DREAMS – ALLMAN BROTHERS,
IN THE GARDEN OF EDEN – I. RON BUTTERFLY

RIVER QUOTE…
CRAIGO: "IT'S BETTER THAN A STICK UP YOUR
BUM" *WHAT IS?* CRAIGO: "ANYTHING!"

The Grant River flows through the extreme southwest corner of Wisconsin. It winds in a generally southward direction for 25 miles until it empties into the Mississippi River near the town of Potosi. The river's headwaters begin 10 miles north of Beetown and 10 miles west of Lancaster.

The 5.5 mile Grant River trip detailed in this chapter begins a little northeast of Beetown at the County Road U Bridge. The take out is at the Camel Ridge Road Bridge, southeast of Beetown.

Two points worth noting, from Grant River Canoe & Kayak Rental livery folks…

1) All of the landings on this stretch of the river are private. You can launch anywhere that you want, just not on anyone's stairs.
2) There is great sensitivity among landowners regarding any stopping on their land.

Although there are occasional, very enjoyable, light rapids runs encountered, the Grant River is beginner-paddling friendly.

The fishermen we spoke with were after smallmouth bass, red horse suckers, and carp.

The Grant River canoe & kayak team was Craig Weaks, Chris Weaks, Paul Pienta, Toni LaPorte, Kenny Umphrey, Maggie & Doc. The Grant trip was taken in May.

THE RIVER: PADDLING THE GRANT

You launch at County Road U and end at the Camel Road Bridge. The Grant River width averages 30' on this stretch. The depth varies from bottom-scraping to 3'. Cows drinking from the river, seen 4 minutes downstream from the launch, stopped to watch us float by.

.2 mi/10 min: wrapped around both sides of a midstream island is a fine little rapids run. After 120' of flat water is a real sweet whitewater run. Beautiful rock outcroppings are on the left.

.6 mi/17 min: along the left shore is a 100' tall bluff.

.9 mi/25 min: where the river bends right, you look straight ahead at flat farm country. This will be your surroundings for the next hour.

1.4 mi/38 min: a barn is 200 yards beyond the right bank. In the distance, 3 silos front a high bluff. One minute downstream and on a left bend is a nice and short rapids run. A pretty rock-strewn creek merges from the right.

2.1 mi/52 min: on a left bend is a 30' long stone and sand beach. Around the bend and visible in the distance is a red barn next to a house on a hill.

2.6 mi/1 hr 7 min: the river bends left at a 4-wheeler crossing. Two minutes downstream a big creek (2/3rds the width of the Grant) merges from the right.

3.2 mi/1 hr 24 min: for the first time since the .9 mile mark, one hour ago, you've cleared the flat farm country and are paddling among tall trees.

3.7 mi/1 hr 33 min: gorgeous rock outcroppings are on the right bank. Light rapids run alongside.

3.9 mi/1 hr 37 min: paddle over a 4-wheeler crossing. Turkey buzzards fly above.

4.1 mi/1 hr 40 min: there's a great stone beach break spot on the right.

4.2 mi/1 hr 45 min: as Maggie notes, the rock outcroppings on the left look like 3 whales with beards. Downstream, the outcropping on the left has a Georgia O'Keefe look to it.

4.5 mi/1 hr 54 min: you are floating through rapids. Over your right shoulder is a beautiful red farmhouse. 2 minutes downstream, a 4' wide creek merges from the right. The river's current is now very slow – but not for long…

4.8 mi/2 hrs 2 min: light rapids take you past another fine looking rock outcropping. One minute later, a stone island angles down into the river from the right shore, squeezing the Grant and creating a great little rapids run. Behind the island is a beautiful little spring.

5.6 miles/2 hours 19 minutes: you're in! After passing beneath the Camel Ridge Road, take out on the right shore. Just before you pull over are some fun rapids to float through.

THE TOWN: BEETOWN

Green Bay Packer local radio station affiliate: WGLR-AM 1280
Milwaukee Brewer local radio station affiliate: WGLR-FM 97.7

Beetown was founded in 1827, 21 years before Wisconsin was granted statehood. Its population is a little over 700. Lead mining was a key Beetown employer from the early to the mid 1800s. Lead mines could be found everywhere in the area, and are still fun spots to explore today. One such fun spot is 30 minutes east of Beetown at *The Mining Museum* in the town Platteville. This museum offers an underground tour of the 1845 Bevans Lead Mine (you'll go 90 steps down into the mine where it's 52 degrees year 'round), an above ground ride on a 1931 mine train, and provides an education on the history of lead and zinc mining in southwestern Wisconsin.

Formerly located in Beetown, but since moved 25 miles east to Platteville, is *The Rollo Jamison Museum*. Rollo Jamison was born on a farm in Beetown in 1899. From his days as a child picking up arrowheads in a field at his family's farm, Rollo developed a love of collecting just about anything and everything. When he opened a tavern in Beetown in 1941, he filled the place with items that he had acquired over the years. In his bar he would talk history with anyone who had stories to tell. He soon bought a wire recorder and began recording oral history interviews. Rollo sold his tavern in the early 1950s and used the money to buy land & build a Beetown museum. Besides these recorded histories – some of the earliest wire recordings ever made – his museum housed the wide & varied items he collected over the years, including fascinating ones such as Abe Lincoln's liquor license (perhaps an Honest Abe fallback plan should the election of 1864 go poorly).

In order to keep the museum alive after he had passed on, Rollo and some friends made arrangements to move his museum from Beetown to Platteville. Rollo Jamison's passing and the move to Platteville both occurred in 1981. Today, the Rollo Jamison Museum and the Mining Museum sit side-by-side at the eastern end of Platteville's Downtown Historic District. For information, call (608) 348-3301 or click on www.mining.jamison.museum.

Nine miles southwest of Beetown, and along the banks of the Mississippi River, is the town of Cassville. There you can take a trip back in time to the 1800s with a visit to Stonefield, the 2,000 acre estate of Wisconsin's first governor, Nelson Dewey. One newspaper of the day described Stonefield as "the showplace of Wisconsin with its beautiful green lawns, gardens and orchards, stables and other buildings, and miles of stone fences." On the grounds of the estate sat the governor's 1868 home, with a view in the distance of the Mississippi River. Today, a trip to Stonefield allows you to re-visit the 1860s through the 30 buildings that make up the Stonefield Village and Wisconsin's largest collection of farm tools and machinery from the state's agricultural past. Stonefield is at 12195 Highway VV (off WI-133) in Cassville 53806. Call (608) 725-5210.

When paddling the Grant River, there is no camping in Beetown. Nearby camping is located at the Whitetail Bluff Camp & Resort. Whitetail is at 8973 Irish Ridge Road in Cassville. Call (608) 725-5577.

If you decide to float the Grant all the way until it flows into the Mississippi River, you may want to look into camping at the Grant River Recreation Area, 2 miles south of Potosi off Highway 133 along the Mississippi River. Potosi is called the "Catfish Capital of Wisconsin" and fishing for channel catfish is big fun along this part of the Mississippi.

The Grant River Recreation Area is next to one of Wisconsin's greatest archeological finds: a large Native American burial site on the banks of the Mississippi, estimated to be 1,000 years old, of the Woodland tribe. Call for camping reservations at 1-877-444-6777.

THE TAVERN: GRATTAN'S VALLEY TAP

The guest book at Grattan's has been signed by folks from as far away as England. If you've ever had a meal in England, you'll know why they travel so far for a good burger.

Better make that, to quote my niece, a ginormously good burger. A burger that is 3 times larger than the size of the large bun that it is served on. A burger that was big enough to feed the 3 of us, and then some. Paul asked for his burger well done. Owner Roger replied that his burgers come two ways, froze or done. Paul said he'd like his done.

As you're getting ready to enter Grattan's, you're greeted by a neon Old Milwaukee sign out front. Inside, Pabst Blue Ribbon longnecks are on hand, always a sure sign of quality.

The rustic main bar has a dance floor, which you may want to use to high step to the fine tunes on the tavern's juke box. An outdoor party pavilion is attached to the bar.

All Grattan's tables have built-in, coaster-sized, wooden beer holders, 6" below the table top so as not to interfere with your card game. Now there's some good thinkin'. If you're ever in a tavern in London, and you see built-in, coaster-sized, wooden beer coasters, 6" below the table top, you'll know where they got the idea from.

Grattan's Valley Tap is located at 7809 County Road U (just south of 81) in Beetown.

Sources: Grant River Canoe & Kayak Rentals, www.wisconsinhistory.org, The Mining Museum & Rollo Jamison Museum, Wisconsin Historical Society, Mississippi River Project

KICKAPOO RIVER

ONTARIO, WI
TRIP 6.6 MILES & 2 HOURS 22 MINUTES LONG

BEGINNER ABILITY

LIVERY: **DRIFTY'S CANOE RENTAL,
HIGHWAY 33 & 131 NORTH,
ONTARIO WI 54651, (608) 337-
4288, WWW.DRIFTYSCANOERENTALNET.
OWNER – TONY KELBEL.**

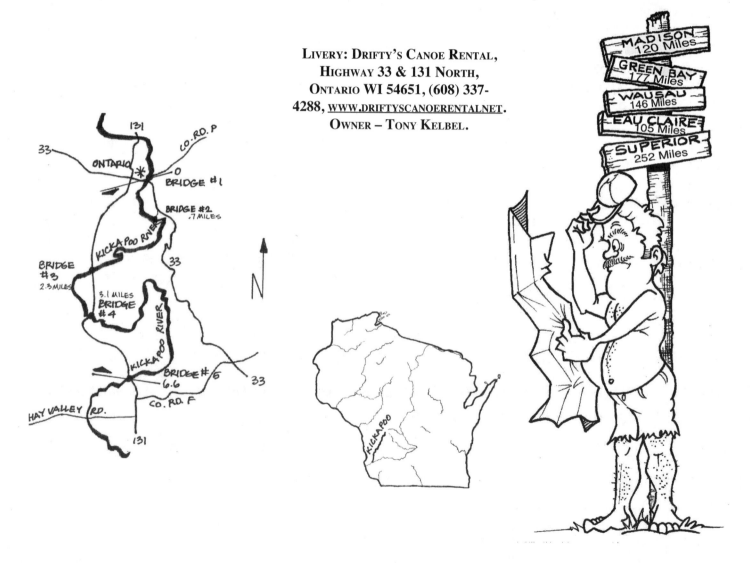

KICKAPOO RIVER

SOUNDTRACK: ROCK CASUAL – THE STAGE-MEN, MOZART
ON ICE – VICTORIA ZANDE, PAPA'S GOT A BRAND NEW
BAG – JAMES BROWN, POLONAISE - FREDERIC CHOPIN,
JAZZMAN – LISA SIMPSON & BLEEDING GUMS MURPHY

RIVER QUOTE…
DOC (ANTICIPATING HUSHED REVERENCE): "KENNY,
HOW WOULD YOU RATE THE KICKAPOO?"
KENNY (AFTER A LONG PAUSE): "WAS THAT
THE ONE WE CANOED YESTERDAY?"

Kickapoo is an Algonquin Indian word meaning, "he who goes here, then there", which refers to the Algonquin-speaking Kickapoo tribe's nomadic wanderings. It is also an appropriate phrase for a stream sometimes referred to as "the crookedest river in the world". Flowing south/southwest for 130 miles from its headwaters near Wilton, the Kickapoo eventually empties into the Wisconsin River near Wauzeka. From Wauzeka, it's 17 river miles until the Wisconsin River flows into the Mississippi River. The Wisconsin is the longest river in the Badger State, and the Kickapoo River is its longest tributary.

Chris' comment that "this is the most beautiful river I've ever been on" found no one in disagreement. The fabulous rock outcroppings come at you one after the other (there are 12 separate outcroppings on this short trip), and each one is stunning in its beauty.

The outcroppings provide a unique window into our long ago past. Millions of years ago, the valley where the Kickapoo flows today did not exist. The sandstone and shale rock layers along each side of the river were continuous layers that stretched across where the river now flows. Over time, erosion cut through these geological layers, leaving a deep valley for the Kickapoo to flow through, and dazzling rock outcroppings for paddlers to view on each side of the water.

Later, during the Ice Age, glaciers deposited vast amounts of sediment called "drift" on the landscape which would have eroded or flatten the rock outcroppings. However, the Kickapoo River sits in a pocket of southwest Wisconsin known as the "driftless region", i.e. the area is unglaciated, meaning that the glaciers - and the erosion that they would've brought – bypassed the area. Since there were no glaciers to change the natural course of the river, it's thought by geologists that the Kickapoo is one of the world's oldest river systems. And, with no glacial drift deposited, the beautiful Kickapoo River sandstone & shale outcroppings remain to this day a visual blessing to us all.

Once folks experience the Kickapoo, it's hard to get 'em to stay away. Historians believe that indigenous people used this area as a summer getaway for over 7,000 years. In this locale, the indigenous people would be the Ho-Chunk Nation. The Ho-Chunks are also known as the Winnebago tribe, which brings to mind a wonderful mental image of Native Americans in large, white recreational vehicles, pulling up to the riverside and getting ready to have themselves a fine weekend rendezvous.

The Kickapoo Kanoo Team was Chris Weaks, Craig Weaks, Bret Holbrook, Kenny Umphrey, & Doc

THE RIVER: PADDLING THE KICKAPOO

Launch from in front of Drifty's Canoe Rental in Ontario, 50' upstream from the Highway 33 Bridge, also known as Kickapoo Bridge number 1. The trip ends at Kickapoo bridge number 5. Each bridge is clearly marked with numbers 1 – 5.

At the launch point, the river is 25' wide and 2' deep. Over the course of the trip, the river runs between 1' to 2' deep and between 15' to 30' wide. Immediately upon the launch, you float through mild rapids.

.2 mi/6 min: on the right bank, float past the first rock outcropping – the first of many – seen today.

.5 mi/12 min: the rock outcropping on the right is cantilevered over the river, with pine trees growing out of the outcropping's rocky top.

.7 mi/18 min: pass beneath Kickapoo Bridge number 2.

1 mi/27 min: as the river bends right, a take-a-break-friendly dirt slope welcomes you to the right shore. Across the river on the left bank is a gorgeous outcropping.

1.1 mi/30 min: the river drops, rushing you through short rapids for a fun little kick!
Another 1/10th of a mile downstream is a sandy beach at the right bend, across the stream from a rock outcropping.

1.8 mi/45 min: paddle past a stone island that sits midstream. Two minutes beyond the island, beautiful whitewater takes you downstream for 2/10ths of a mile. The whitewater ends at sandy beaches on both banks.

2.3 mi/1 hour: Kickapoo Bridge number 3.

3 mi/1 hr 10 min: after the river bends right, visible directly in front of you are 80' tall majestic rock outcroppings on both shores.

3.1 mi/1 hr 11 min: Kickapoo Bridge number 4. Three minutes beyond sits a left bend rock outcropping.

3.7 mi/1 hr 22 min: on the right is the spectacular sight of an outcropping with 3 side-by- side-by-side protrusions extending out into the Kickapoo.

4 mi/1 hr 30 min: large rock outcropping, right bank.

4.6 mi/1 hr 40 min: drop-dead gorgeous (yeah, another) rock outcropping at the end of a straightaway as the river bends right.

5.1 mi/1 hr 52 min: 400' high castle-upon-a-hill-like rock outcropping. It is high-in-the-sky beauty.

5.8 mi/2 hrs 5 min: State Park on the left with boat ramp, a big pavilion, picnic tables and restrooms.

6 mi/2 hrs 11 min: the left shore outcropping has a pirates cove that you can paddle into. We've christened these "kissing rocks".

6.6 mi/2 hrs 22 min: arrive at Kickapoo Bridge number 5, exit on the left.

THE TOWN: ONTARIO

Green Bay Packer local radio station affiliate: WKTY-AM 580
Milwaukee Brewer local radio station affiliate: WKTY-AM 580

Ontario, Wisconsin – 467 beautiful folks and 1 beautiful river. Wonderfully, the modern day history of the town began with a canoe trip down the Kickapoo River. In 1842, Esau Johnson first visited the area and loved what he saw. He went to work building a canoe. (Drifty's Canoe Rental being not yet open), and soon paddled his new boat downstream, returning with family and friends who went to work building Ontario. Esau's son Lewis was the first non-native American born in the county.

Ontario provided economic benefits to its earliest settlers. Its location at the junction of the Kickapoo River and Brush Creek made it the ideal spot to establish grist mills (for turning wheat into flour). The intersection of these two waterways was

heavily wooded, providing a prime area for cutting trees & floating the lumber downstream to feed the 1800's western settlement of the mostly treeless prairies in neighboring Iowa.

Ontario's setting along the banks of the Kickapoo has been a both a blessing and a curse for its residents. Terrible flooding has been a regular occurrence. The steep sandstone walls along the riverbanks do not absorb water, so rainfall drives up river levels quickly. In addition, the Kickapoo has over 140 tributaries. During heavy rainfalls these tributaries send a tremendous volume of water to the river, and flooding results. Ontario's worst flood took place in 1907 as folks celebrated the 50th anniversary of the town's 1857 founding. Lighting and tornadoes pounded the area, spiking the heavy rains ("A waterfall that would make Niagara look like a trickle" a local newspaper reported). The lumbering boom of the late-1800s had stripped the nearby hills of their forest cover, allowing the severe rains to cascade down the hillsides and on into the valleys, where the normally placid creeks feeding the Kickapoo sent a tidal wave of water to the river. The now greatly-swollen Kickapoo went well over its banks, uprooting trees and knocking down buildings. The rampaging river ripped the old wooden covered bridge from its moorings, turning it into a high-speed battering ram that slammed into the new steel bridge, flipping it completely upside down.

A look at the history of Ontario and the Kickapoo River refers to devastating floods in 1907, 1935, 1944, 1951, etc.

etc. These reoccurrences were the driving force behind the *La Farge Project*, an effort at flood control in the Kickapoo Valley. Working together, the Army Corps of Engineers and the Wisconsin Conservation Department in 1959 began planning a dam and an 800-acre reservoir for that section of the Kickapoo River north of the town of La Farge and south of Ontario (2 towns 14 miles apart). With the 1962 Flood Control Act, the U.S. Congress authorized $15 million to cover the projected cost. As La Farge Project plans developed over time, boosting tourism became as big a part of the goal as did flood control, including creation of a 1,780 acre lake to entice vacationers to the area. From a proposed dam one mile north of La Farge, the lake would extend 12 miles upstream, putting much of the Kickapoo River underwater, including bridge 5 (this chapter's take out point). In the valley downstream from bridge 5, trees now along the riverbank would've been below the lake's surface.

In 1969, the Army Corps of Engineers began the purchase of 8,600 acres of land for the project. Ontario property was included, even though the northern shores of the lake would've been south of town, since the town would've been in the project's flood plain. Although fair market value was given to 149 rural landowners between La Farge and Ontario, many understandably did not want to leave homes or farms that they loved. All homes, farms, and other structures on the 8,600 acres were eventually torn down.

In 1974, the brakes were put on the project. The governor requested an environmental review, conducted by the University of Wisconsin. The review suggested that the dam would negatively impact the environment and that the lake water quality would suffer over time, ending the hoped for tourism boost. Another two decades of studies and debate would pass before a 1996 return of the project land from the federal government to the State of Wisconsin and the Bureau of Indian Affairs, with 1,200 of the 8,600 acres held in a trust for the state's original tenants, the Ho-Chunk Indian Nation. This led to a 1997 "Memorandum of Understanding" and joint management of the land between the State of Wisconsin & the Ho-Chunk Nation.

In the end, the La Farge Project was cancelled, sporadic and sometimes deadly flooding from the Kickapoo River spilling over its banks continues, people who didn't want to sell were forced out of their homes and farms needlessly, and strong anti-government feeling in the area runs high to this day. Although the 12 mile long lake was never created and carloads of vacationers to visit the lake never materialized, tourism in the area is doing very well. Those 8,600 acres between La Farge and Ontario that would've been the La Farge Project is instead a protected recreation area known as the Kickapoo Valley Reserve, a popular tourist destination offering hunting, hiking, camping, horseback riding, spectacular views (check out Wildcat Mountain), fishing (some of the finest trout fishing in the Midwest) and, of course, canoeing the Kickapoo River.

Accessible just ten minutes north of Ontario is our nation's first "rails to trails" hiking & biking trail, the Elroy-Sparta State Trail. Formally opened to the public in 1967, the trail runs east to west for 32 miles along the abandoned Chicago & North Western Railroad bed. Trail travelers are provided the added bonus of winding through 3 rock train tunnels, two 1/4 mile long each and the third 3/4s of a mile long. Along the Elroy-Sparta Trail's 32 miles, you'll cross over 34 old railroad bridges, each having been planked over with protective side railings installed.

One of the great stories from Ontario's history revolves around how they obtained their Community Hall. The story begins 38 miles west of Ontario, along the Mississippi River in the town of La Crosse. In 1938, the folks in charge wanted to widen a channel in the Mississippi River. In order for this widening to happen, a dance hall on Goose Island, just south of La

Crosse, needed to be removed and was put up for sale. Ontario folks got wind of this, and it just so happened that they needed a new Community Hall. A price of $500 was negotiated with the federal government, and a deal was struck. 4 carpenters dismantled the dance hall, and Ontario residents pitched in with their time and trucks to haul and reassemble the building back home. When funding to complete the project ran short, residents voted overwhelmingly to pass the hat and take over ownership.

Fast forward half a century later. In 1988, there was talk of tearing the Community Hall down, since the old dance hall was showing its age. A fella named Jim Bavetta defended the old girl, convincing town folk that not only did they need this gathering spot, but that taking her down would betray those who with their efforts, time and trucks disassembled the building, moved it 38 miles, and then reassembled it back home 50 years earlier. Jim's words struck a chord, and since 1988 money has been invested as improvements of the old hall are needed.

In a town where so many had to sell their homes and land, painfully and against their wishes, for the ill-fated La Farge Project, it was probably inevitable that they would do whatever they could to keep a structure near and dear to their hearts for so many years like the Community Hall. Jim Bavetta, who reminded the residents why the Hall was important to them, was one of those folks who had to sell his property for the La Farge Project. Jim's Cozy Nook Café, a favorite Ontario gathering spot after WWII, was bought by the feds and torn down because it sat in the Project floodplain. Before the Cozy Nook Cafe was dismantled, it sat right across the street… from the Community Hall.

Area camping is available at Wildcat State Park. From the park's heights are hiking trails that offer spectacular views of the Kickapoo Valley. The park's 3,603 mostly wooded acres contain 25 miles of hiking trails, 17 miles of snowshoeing trails, 15 miles of horse trails, 7 miles of cross-country ski trails, and a 1.3 mile interpretive nature trail. Wildcat Mountain has a nature center and interpretive program, picnic facilities, and opportunities for bird and wildlife watching, and fishing, too.

Wildcat State Park is at E13660 State Highway 33, Ontario 54651. Call (608) 337-4775.

THE TAVERN: RIVER'S END BAR

314 Main Street, Ontario WI 54651; (608) 337-4803

Walking into River's End, you're immediately welcomed by the Pabst Blue Ribbon Beer neon guitar sign hanging on the wall… home sweet home. So wonderfully small town ("don't worry about where you park, the police aren't working tonight") and cozy, the River's End makes for a fine place to relax after a great day on the Kickapoo. Although clearly the strangers in this pub, we were made to feel at home by the regulars, as they shared their morel mushroom hunting success stories with us, and cheered along while we watched our hockey team on the bar's TV. After a half an hour of enthusiastically shouting alongside us, a local turned to me and asked, "Now _which ones_ are the Red Wings?" To quote Vid, "they don't know Red Wings from chicken wings", but there they were hollering right along side us, God bless 'em.

If the bar conversation isn't enough, River's End has a juke box, darts, video games and a pool table. These folks can cook, too: River's End pizza & burgers made everyone fat 'n happy in the evening, and next morning breakfast made for a mighty fine start to the day.

Chapter sources: Always the River by Karen Parker, Wisconsin Department of Natural Resources, The Kickapoo Valley Association, Wikipedia, Drifty's owner Tony Kelbel, Jarrod Roll from the Monroe County Local History Museum

106

LEMONWEIR RIVER

MAUSTON, WI
TRIP 3.6 MILES & 1 HOURS 43 MINUTES LONG

BEGINNER ABILITY

LIVERY: COUNTRY CRUISIN' KAYAKS & CANOES, 807 DIVISION STREET, MAUSTON WI 53948, (608) 548-4280. OWNER BARBARA BAKER.

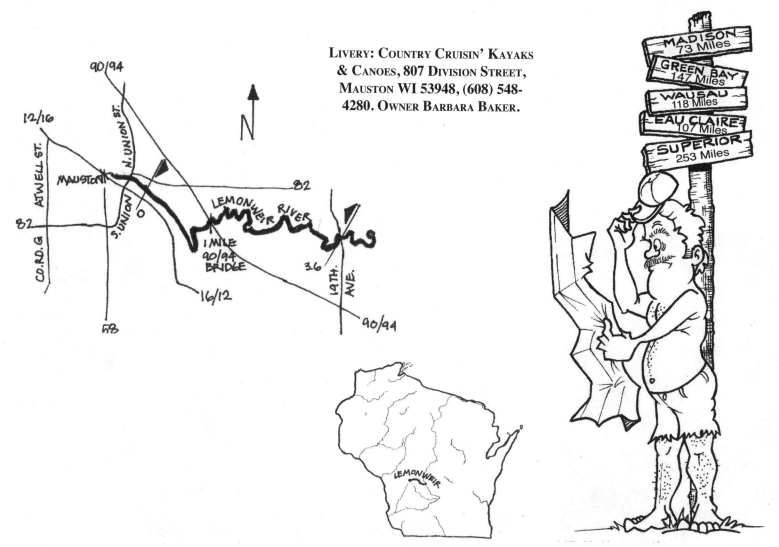

THE BACKGROUND: LEMONWEIR RIVER

SOUNDTRACK: THE VOODOO WALK – THE VOODOOS, TAKE ME TO THE RIVER – THE USUALS W/ THE FABULOUS SANDY, TEMPEST – CLAUDIO ARRAU (BEETHOVEN), THE RIVER HYMN – THE BAND, IKO IKO – THE GRATEFUL DEAD

RIVER QUOTE…
KIM ERIKSEN: "NEVER GRAB A TREE BRANCH WHEN YOU'RE IN A MOVING CANOE"

"Le-mo-we" was the name given to the river by a Native American camping along side it in the 1800s. While there, the Indian dreamed that he lost his wampum (money sack) and the location of the loss. When he awoke, the man traveled to the location indicated in the dream and found his wampum. The name means "the river of memories".

The Lemonweir River runs southeast for 15 miles from Mauston until it empties into the Wisconsin River. This river junction is just upstream from the Wisconsin Dells. The Lemonweir is a slow moving body of water. Even after a recent spring rain, our little flotilla paddled at less than 2 miles an hour.

The slow pace of the Lemonweir makes it beginner friendly and a good choice for a fun family float. Please note, however, that this is a deep river in many spots, and a slow pace doesn't mean that canoes and kayaks can't tip over in it (thus Kim's river quote, "Never grab a branch when you're in a moving canoe"). All Lemonweir River paddlers should wear life vests. For fishin' folks, Sturgeon, Northern Pike, and brown trout are plentiful.

Country Crusin' Kayaks & Canoes offers their customers four Lemonweir River trips:

(1)   the 2-hour float featured in this chapter, launching from below the Mauston Dam to the 19th Avenue Bridge (aka Lemonweir Mills),

(2)   a 2nd 2-hour float, launching at the 19th Avenue Bridge to the HH Bridge,

(3)   a day-long trip combining trips 1 and 2, and

(4)   a 10-hour paddle that covers the 15 miles of the Lemonweir from Mauston all the way to the mouth of the Wisconsin River.

Paddling the Lemonweir was Neal Linkon, Pete & Peggy Armstrong, George, Susan & Katie Mutert, Kim & Julie Eriksen, Maggie & Doc. The trip was in May.

THE RIVER: PADDLING THE LEMONWEIR

Launch just downstream from the Mauston Dam, at what used to be the site of an old glass factory. This access is referred to locally as "the farm".

As you begin your Lemonweir trip, the river is 70' wide, slow-moving, over 6' deep mid-stream, and you're on a long straightaway. 500' downstream and on the right bank, water gushes out at the base of a concrete culvert. 50' beyond the culvert, a creek merges from the right.

.4 mi/14 min: the river bends left as a creek rolls in from the right.

.5 mi/17 min: the Lemonweir makes a big loop to the left. From the right and flowing beneath a bridge, One Mile Creek, a brown trout stream, merges from your right. Since the river and the creek are both moving so slowly, there may be confusion (there was within our group) whether to paddle right and go beneath the bridge or paddle left. Paddle left to stay on the river.

1 mi/31 min: you'll know that you're exactly one mile into the trip when you float beneath the Highway 90/94 Bridge.

1.4 mi/42 min: at the upstream end of an island, follow the current left.

2 mi/1 hr 8 min: the first home seen on this stretch of the Lemonweir is on the right, shortly before paddling under power lines.

2.4 mi/1 hr 15 min: a creek merges from the right, rich with Northern Pike.

2.7 mi/1 hr 24 min: another creek rolls in from the right.

3.6 mi/1 hr 43 min: you're in! Exit the river on the right shore on Country Cruisin's property, one bend before the 19th Avenue Bridge, also known as Lemonweir Mills.

THE TOWN: MAUSTON

Green Bay Packer local radio station affiliate: WRDB-AM 1400
Milwaukee Brewer local radio station affiliate: WBDL-FM 102.9

Are you one of those who wander
To some cool and shady nook,
With your pole and line for fishing
There to drop an idle hook?

If you love old nature's beauty
Where the blue sky and a cloud
Seem to float upon the ripples
And the birds sing extra loud.

Try your luck someday I ask you
Where the river smoothly glides
Just below the splashing waters
Of the dam, at even tide,

There the flowers grow in the wild wood
And so tall the elms seem,
Their reflection on the water
Spell one like an enchanted dream,

If you look around for beauty
And you want your dreams fulfilled
Spend an afternoon a fishing
By the old "Lemonweir Mill"

Down By The Lemonweir Mill by Vada M. Dixon

The site of what once was the Lemonweir Mill is where this chapter's float down the Lemonweir River comes to an end. At this location in 1852, a mill dam was built for the first grist (flouring) mill in Juneau County. Around the mill, the town of Lemonweir was born, a platted village designed with hopes of overshadowing nearby Mauston. Those hopes were dashed in 1857 when the railroad line was laid running through Mauston.

Prior to the Europeans arrival, the area around what would become known as Mauston was populated primarily by the Winnebago Indians, also known as the Ho-Chunk tribe. These tribesmen traversed the Lemonweir in dugout, or pirogue (pee-row), canoes cut from white pine logs and waterproofed with pine pitch. Later, they floated the water in birch bark canoes.

The town of Mauston was born in 1848, plotted by General M. Maughs, a veteran of the Indian Wars. The General ran a mill in the area, and the town soon became known as Maughs Mill, then Maughstown, which eventually corrupted its way into "Mauston".

By 1868, another grist mill in town achieved notoriety by being ranked among the finest in the land. That mill was operated by Ben Boorman. His home, known as the Boorman House, was built in 1877 and still stands today as a wonderful piece of living history.

Located at 211 North Union, the Boorman House now is home to the Juneau County Historical Society and the Mauston archives. On display in the rooms of the house are artifacts from the late-1800s, including furniture, toiletries, period clothing, and a 38-star American flag. A curved mahogany staircase takes you to the second floor. Marble fireplaces grace each of three rooms. The roof is adorned with a "widow's walk". The Boorman House is open to the public Sat and Sun 1PM to 4PM Memorial Day to Labor Day, and anytime by appointment 608-847-4450.

"River of Memories Rendezvous" is an annual pre-1840s re-enactment held in Mauston along the Lemonweir River. The gathering commemorates the story of the traveling Indian who, while camped along the river, dreamed that he lost his wampum (i.e. money sack) as well as the location of the lost wampum. When he awoke, the man traveled to the location indicated in the dream and found his wampum, and promptly named the river "Le-Mo-We", or "the river of memories". The annual "River of Memories Rendezvous" replicates mid-1800s life through a village of tepees, with campfire cooking, period clothing and merchants. Buck skinners and re-enactors add to the historic feel through lifestyle demonstrations, an exhibition of outdoor skills of the bygone time, and the establishment of a functioning fur trader's camp

The Lemonweir River flows into the Wisconsin River just a little northeast of the town of Lyndon Station. During a 1880s week-long church mission in the town, 1,200 people took the pledge never to take another drop of alcohol. Soon after, many of these pledgers marched over to Leo's Tavern, where they lifted their glasses with a toast to their pledge. An inquiry over the years at Lyndon Station asks, "We're taking benediction at Leo's. Are you with us?"

Area camping is available at Castle Rock County Park on Highway G in Mauston. Castle Rock Lake is the 4th largest inland lake in Wisconsin, and you can have some fun fishing and boating near your campsite. Call (608) 847-7089.

THE TAVERN: CARL'S BRIGHT SPOT

Opened around 1910, Carl's Bright Spot sits in downtown Mauston at the corner of Union and State Streets, very near the Mauston Dam. Back in the early 1900s, the east half of the bar, where the pool table now sits, was a barber shop.

Carl passed on and his son Rob now owns the bar. It's a comfortable place filled with a lot of caring folks who pitch in to help people whether they're fellow regulars or not. One such effort is an annual event that's been running for 20 years or so: Carl's sponsors the Linda Householder Golf Outing to raise funds for the "Friends & Family Cancer Foundation" which helps folks with their medical bills and miscellaneous expenses.

Carl's does not have a grill, but besides cold beer and other drinks, the tavern offers its visitors a juke box, darts, video games and a pool table.

Not much has changed at the bar with the ownership passing from Carl to Rob. Well, maybe one thing has based on a sign posted on the tavern wall:

Notice – as of June 8, 2009 the credit department at Carl's Bright Spot is closed – please do not ask the bartenders for loans & please feel free to pay back all outstanding loans as soon as possible. Thank you for your cooperation.   Signed, Rob

Carl's Bright Spot is at 419 East State Street, and their phone no. is (608) 847-4002.

Sources: Barbara Baker, Rose Clark, Juneau County Visitors Bureau, Wisconsin Historical Collections, Vada M. Dixon, www. castlerockpetenwell.com

LITTLE WOLF RIVER

New London, WI
Trip 4.3 miles & 2 hours 15 minutes long

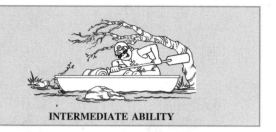

INTERMEDIATE ABILITY

LIVERY: WOLF RIVER TRIPS & CAMPGROUNDS, E8041 COUNTY ROAD X, NEW LONDON WI 54961, (920) 982-2458, WWW.WOLFRIVERTRIPS.COM. OWNERS MARK FLEASE, GARY FLEASE, & JANET KOPLIEN.

ROYALTON

54

54

LITTLE WOLF RIVER

CO. RD. B

CO. RD. O

OSTRANDER BRIDGE 2.9 MILES

4.3

CO. RD. X

N

LITTLE WOLF

MADISON 117 Miles

GREEN BAY 40 Miles

WAUSAU 75 Miles

EAU CLAIRE 172 Miles

SUPERIOR 303 Miles

THE BACKGROUND: LITTLE WOLF RIVER

SOUNDTRACK: DRY RIVER – DESPERATE OTTOS, MADMAN ACROSS THE WATER – ELTON JOHN (CRYSTAL RIVER TRIBUTE), BYE BYE BLUES – LES PAUL & MARY FORD, BURNING OF THE MIDNIGHT LAMP – JAMES MARSHALL HENDRIX, PIANO SONATA IN F MAJOR - WOLFGANG AMADEUS MOZART

RIVER QUOTE...
PETER: "DO YOU HAVE A LIGHTER IN YOUR DRY BAG?"
DOC: "NO, BUT I HAVE A PICTURE OF LARRY TATE"

The Little Wolf River flows for 27 miles, with its headwaters 30 minutes northeast of Stevens Point, west of the town of Big Falls, and north of County Road C. The Little Wolf begins its journey on a straight line east. Once through Big Falls, the river turns south towards Manawa, slowing briefly for the dam in that town. Arrival at the dam marks the midpoint from the Little Wolf's beginnings until its merger with the Wolf River, a little over 13 miles to Manawa's southeast.

The section of the Little Wolf highlighted in this chapter launches from Highway 54, in the small town of Royalton, and ends at the livery west of New London. As you shove off the riverbank just upstream from the Highway 54 Bridge, you're halfway between Manawa and New London. The river is very shallow here, a harbinger of things to come.

Our trip was in July. In general, unless there is sufficient rainfall, mid-summer on the Little Wolf would be best enjoyed on a kayak or tubing, which was the most popular form of travel during our time on the river. Our canoes were too heavy for the shallow river, and there were a dozen times when we were bottomed out and were forced to get out of the boats and walk them to water deep enough to continue our float. Local wisdom says save the canoes for an April to mid-June river trip.

We were treated to multiple eagle sightings as we paddled downstream. A testament to the health of the Little Wolf was the fact that large schools of walleye & bass swam by us during much of our time on the water. Many rocks dot the river, from palm-sized to 6' in diameter.

The Little Wolf paddlers were Pete & Peggy Armstrong, Kenny Umphrey, Tommy Holbrook, Neal Linkon, Jeff Mitchell, & Doc.

THE RIVER: PADDLING THE LITTLE WOLF

Launch just upstream from the Highway 54 Bridge at Royalton. Take out at the County Road X Bridge at the livery.

Upon launching, the river is 50' wide and there is bottom-scraping immediately. In two minutes you're beneath the bridge and the water is suddenly over-your-paddle deep. Minutes downstream from the bridge the water shallows to a depth of 2'. The first of many rock gardens is 3 minutes into today's trip.

.4 mi/14 min: An island sits left of center. There is a great deal of rocks just below the water's surface, some unseen until your boat is jarred and you're leaning left or right. Much effort is spent working to keep the boats upright.

.7 mi/26 min: the entire width of the river is too shallow to paddle through, forcing today's first canoe walk-through, lasting for 1/20th of a mile.

.9 mi/34 min: 3 eagles fly above, two all white and one brown-gray. They move from tree to tree, until finally perching side by side by side. A wonderful treat!

1.5 mi/48 min: the Little Wolf turns left and becomes a 1/5th of a mile long straight away, one that gives the impression of being completely filled with rocks. The largest rock sits along the left bank and, according to fellow paddler, crack researcher, and part-time bus driver Tommy, "is the size of a bus".

2 mi/1 hr 7 min: where an island sits left of midstream, a beautiful class 1 S-curved rapids runs to the right.

2.2 mi/1 hr 12 min: from the left bank to the right bank, the water is too low to paddle a canoe through.

2.4 mi/1 hr 20 min: paddle into a 1/4 mile long rock garden.

2.9 mi/1 hr 30 min: the Ostrander Bridge is reached. This is the first bridge you paddle beneath since launching at the Highway 54 Bridge, and is the livery starting point for their short tubing trip.

3.3 mi/1 hr 45 min: beyond the right riverbank is a barn with silos.

3.5 mi/1 hr 53 min: an island lays dead center in the Little Wolf. The river widens to 70' and deepens slightly immediately downstream from the island.

BE ALERT!...

4 mi/2 hrs 9 min: you reach today's last island encountered. Passage is blocked to the right. To the left, there is class 1+ rapids, very rocky and with a quick current.

4.3 miles/2 hours 15 minutes: just past the County Road X Bridge, and you're in! Exit the river on the left bank at the sandy slope.

THE TOWN: NEW LONDON

Green Bay Packer local radio station affiliate: WHBY-AM 1150
Milwaukee Brewer local radio station affiliate: WHBY-AM 1150/WAPL-FM 105.7

New London is in eastern section of central Wisconsin, 20 miles NW of Appleton and 40 miles SW of Green Bay. The Little Wolf River merges into the Wolf River on the west edge of the town. With its location along the two rivers, there's plenty of water-themed activity in New London, and in town you'll find multiple boat launches, docks, marinas & bait shops.

Between early-April to late-May is not only a great time to canoe the Little Wolf, but also the time of year that you have a chance to view sturgeon in the Wolf River as it flows through New London. From along the Wolf River Sturgeon Trail during the spawning season, sturgeon up to 6' long can be viewed, but only for the 2 to 3 days after the river temperature rises to 53 degrees. The trail parallels the Wolf River, it is paved, & stretches for one-half of a mile. Besides being the ideal spot to view the impressively big sturgeon, the Wolf River Sturgeon Trail provides you with a nice place to stroll, relax, or throw in a line, with its picnic tables, benches, and fishing platforms. You can view wildlife by walking off the trail on to an adjacent boardwalk that takes you into the nearby marsh.

The New London area includes some of most lush, picturesque farmland that you'll ever see. Particularly appealing is the north-south drive on Highway 110, just to the west and northwest of New London, rolling through the towns of Manawa and Marion as it crosses over the Little Wolf River several times.

In Manawa, detour off of Highway 110 on to County Road N and head east. You'll soon pass a farm silo painted to look like a can of Pabst Blue Ribbon Beer. I can't imagine what says "Welcome to Wisconsin" more than a farm silo painted to look like a can of PBR. Usually, cans of Pabst have printed on them "12 fluid ounces". The farm silo Pabst can reads "1,500 fluid gallons". Better call some friends over to help with this beer.

North of Manawa on Highway 110, and 3.5 miles south of Marion, is a road marker that tells the tale of Potawatomi Chief Waupaca. In the 1850s, the time when the first white men arrived nearby, the Chief lived in the area of the marker. While traveling where the present city of Waupaca is located, Chief Waupaca's fellow tribesmen, angered by the white man's intrusion on their lives and their land, were eager to massacre the small settlement. After much discussion, the Chief was able to convince the Potawatomi warriors to spare the settlement. Immediately after remounting his horse to continue on his way, the Chief fell dead. Near the site of this Highway 110 road marker are buried Chief Waupaca, his sons, and at least 16 other relatives.

Ten miles south of New London runs the path of what, in 1912, became the USA's first cross-country highway, the Yellowstone Trail. Running along, in part, what today is Highway 10, the Trail was the first highway that could take folks from the east coast to the west as far as Yellowstone Park. Private citizens and motoring clubs worked to improve their local roads that were in the path of the Trail. Roads were connected, and the route was marked with yellow and black paint on fence posts, trees, and large rocks – anything that was big and visible. When the Yellowstone Trail was opened in 1912, it was unpaved and had no numerical markings. Over the next few years, the dirt road was upgraded to a gravel road. In 1918, Wisconsin became the first town, state or country anywhere in the world to identify roads with numbered signs, including those of the Yellowstone Trail. In 1929, the section of the Yellowstone Trail running through Wisconsin was paved in concrete, the first such road that ran completely across the state.

THE TAVERN: UPPER DECK BAR & GRILL

After a day floating down the Little Wolf River, kicking back at the Upper Deck is about as convenient as you can get, sitting right upstairs from the Wolf River Trips livery itself. Our waitress, and family member of the livery owners, Ashley Flease, was excellent.

All 7 members of our Little Wolf expedition team unanimously agreed that the Upper Deck Bar Burgers were incredible. No condiments were used by any of us, as we knew the taste could not be improved on. "Among the best I've *ever* had!" was the consensus.

The tavern has plenty of seating both indoor and out, with some of the outdoor seating providing an excellent view of the river.

May you be as fortunate as we were on your next visit to the Upper Deck Bar & Grill. We met a bar regular named Slippery Bill, a fellow who told us he is, among other things, a hurricane chaser. Slippery Bill was sporting a tshirt that read, "I am not drunk – I am by nature a loud, friendly, clumsy person". We didn't notice any clumsiness from Bill, but 2 out of 3 ain't bad. And, there's probably a fair chance that Bill owns more than one of these tshirts.

Bill was so entertaining, and waitress Ashley did such a great job keeping our drinks and food comin', as well as telling her own stories, we didn't even notice if the Upper Deck Bar & Grill had a pool table, or darts, or video games, or any other such bar diversions.

If you visit the Upper Deck and Slippery Bill and Ashley are around, you probably won't notice either.

Sources: New London Tourism guide, the Yellowstone Trail brochure, the Waupaca Chamber of Commerce

MECAN RIVER

PRINCETON, WI
TRIP 7.0 MILES & 2 HOURS 40 MINUTES LONG

BEGINNER ABILITY

LIVERY: MECAN RIVER OUTFITTERS, W720 STATE ROAD 23, PRINCETON WI 54968, (920) 295-3439, WWW.MECANRIVEROUTFITTERS. COM. OWNERS PAUL & LEANNE HARVEY. THE LIVERY PUTS PADDLERS OUT ON BOTH THE MECAN RIVER AND THE FOX RIVER.

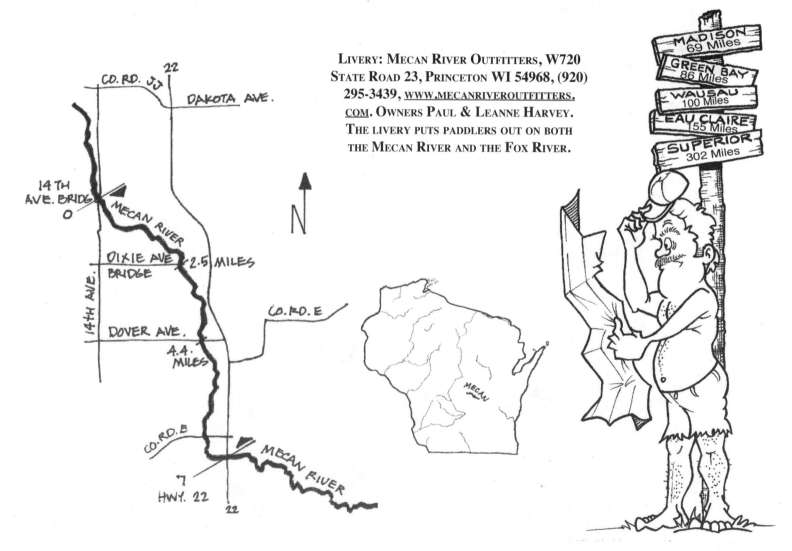

THE BACKGROUND: MECAN RIVER

SOUNDTRACK: GROUND SPEED – MECAN RIVER RAMBLERS, FABER COLLEGE THEME, TRACKIN' – THE ZAKONS, LAND HO! – THE DOORS, BETTER OFF BROKE – DANNY SCHMIDT

RIVER QUOTES:
DOC: "THE RIVER NEVER LIES"

The Mecan (pronounced Ma-can) River is one of the most enjoyable rivers I've ever floated. The river runs south/southeast for 30 miles until it flows into the Fox River.

The Mecan is narrow, usually 15' to 20' wide, and has a spirited current that moves with deceptively quick speed. Your paddling skills get a nice workout on the frequent tight turns and as you work your way around the plentiful deadwood or leaning trees that partially obstruct the water's flow.

In this very windy stream, lead boats are often seen across the lowland brush as they head in the opposite direction, at times as close as 20' away from you. Even when the low brush gives way to trees on the banks, you can still see through the trees to boats going in the other direction on the serpentine turns.

As you approach yet another small farm bridge, you begin to wonder if you can lie down in your canoe or kayak low enough to get under this next one. For those of you who like to combine a little fishing with your floating, the Mecan has a well-earned reputation as a great trout stream.

The Harvey Family has owned & operated the Mecan River Outfitters since 1984, long enough to gain a wealth of knowledge and experiences of the area. Paul Harvey shared some of that wealth with us…

According to Paul, the Mecan Springs, at the river's headwaters, is the location of the highest quality water in the

Midwest. Perrier has been rebuffed in their attempts to buy and bottle the spring waters. A wildlife refuge has been established at the headwaters.

Q: Paul, in all of your years running this business, what memorable event stands out?

A: Well, I was waiting to pick up a couple at the end of their canoe trip. When they floated in, they were completely naked. It was a guy and a gal… said that they ran into some bushes and came out without any of their clothes… still had their pads and paddles. The fella had a single gold tooth (think of the bartender in "Three Amigos") and seemed fairly drunk. He was lying on the bottom of the canoe while the lady was in back paddling above her prone partner. The guy was barely conscious and kept telling me that he had a very, very good time. We loaned them some clothes to go home in.

Q: Paul, after that story, I gotta ask you if there are any other memorable moments?

A: The Long Branch Bar has had a humongous 5-pound burger called "the Hippo" ever since a 1993 incident. A fella kept some exotic animals fenced in near the Budsin Bridge. A camel, a bit of a scamp, bent down and with his teeth pulled the pin out of the gate that held the hippo in. The hippo got loose and was spotted along the riverbank, and had to be put down. The camel was the lone survivor among the animals in the story, probably regaling his friends with the tale over and over in the years since.

Mecan River Outfitters offers 15 different Mecan River trips and two on the Fox River. In a very nice touch, MRO loans dry bags to the unprepared. They also offer a beautiful 5-bedroom lodge with a 35' fieldstone fireplace. The lodge has its own bar with a heavy paddling-themed emphasis. Carved into the bar's u-shaped surface is the outline of the entire 30 miles of the Mecan, beautifully done with all of the bridges clearly noted.

Paddling the Mecan were Neal Linkon, Pete & Peggy Armstrong, Maggie & Doc. The trip was taken in May.

THE RIVER: PADDLING THE MECAN

The suggested trip launches at the 14th Avenue Bridge and takes out at Highway 22.

The Mecan begins 15' wide, 3' deep, and is very marshy with tall grass along the banks.

1 mi/25 min: forest primeval briefly replaces the open, bright surroundings.

1.5 mi/36 min: on the right as the river bends left, the first house today appears.

2.1 mi/52 min: on a right bank bluff is a beautiful log home.

2.3 mi/55 min: float beneath a footbridge with minimal clearance.

2.4 mi/1 hr: as river bends left, an old house on the right is fronted by wooden pilings.

2.5 mi/1 hr 3 min: flow below the Dixie Avenue Bridge through a culvert that is so wide and comfortable that it is reminiscent of when Cosmo Kramer adopted a highway and widened the lanes.

3 mi/1 hr 14 min: home on right bank as river bends left.

3.3 mi/1 hr 20 min: Chaffee Creek moves quickly as it merges from the right. Chaffee is 20' wide at its mouth, adding significant volume to the Mecan, widening the river to 30'.

4.2 mi/1 hr 40 min: a 5' long wooden bridge connects an island to the left shore as the river bends right. The current pushes you hard left at this right bend. Waiting for me in the left bank brush is a 18" long snake, 3" thick, winding itself 5 times around branches leaning out into the Mecan, and sitting about 1' from my eye. Yikes!

4.4 mi/1 hr 45 min: paddle beneath the Dover Avenue Bridge.

4.6 mi/1 hr 50 min: a long creek merges from the right. Then you'll pass below today's first farm bridge. During our early season journey, the clearance is just over 2' from the top of the canoe to the bottom of the bridge.

5 mi/1 hr 57 min: on the right bank sits a house with an apron of large rocks. Immediately downstream is the second farm bridge followed by a farm with 4 silos on the right.

5.4 mi/2 hrs 6 min: third farm bridge – beware of its low-hanging metal cables.

5.6 mi/2 hrs 11 min: float beneath the fourth farm bridge.

6 mi/2 hrs 20 min: fine looking home on the left bank precedes congested low-hanging branches that present a fun challenge to your paddling skills.

6.2 mi/2 hrs 25 min: County E Bridge - paddle through one of its two dual culverts.

6.8 mi/2 hrs 37 min: the end is in sight as you paddle below a bridge.

7 miles/2 hours 40 minutes: you're in at the Highway 22 Bridge! Paddle beneath the bridge and take out on the left shore. Looking beyond the left shore is a sign which reads, "miniature horses = 3.6 miles".

THE TOWN: PRINCETON

Green Bay Packer local radio station affiliate: WISS-AM 1100
Milwaukee Brewer local radio station affiliate: WHBY-AM 1150 & WAPL-FM 105.7

The town of Princeton is sitting pretty along the banks of the Fox River, just a few minutes northeast of where the Mecan River merges into the Fox. Princeton was called "Pleasant Valley" by mid-1800s settlers. The town is in the heart of some of Wisconsin's most fertile land, and once known as "the Bean Center of the World". When Princeton was founded in 1849, it was believed that the town would become a center of commerce as a key port along the Upper Fox River, but the water power along this stretch of the Fox was insufficient to support large mills.

It's a vibrant small town, with boatloads (this *is* a paddling book) of activity and friendly faces during our visit. Of course, we did happen to be in town on the day of "Wisconsin's largest weekly outdoor flea market", held every Saturday from April through October. Beyond the flea market, Princeton hums with outdoor activity galore and places where you find handcrafted furniture, books, garden sculptures, hand blown glass, and more total cool than many big towns have. Several Amish communities are located nearby.

In a pretty neat antique (& more) shop called Johnny Crow's, employee Bonnie told Maggie of the "Fox River Heritage Paddle 2010", which follows the 190-mile length of the Fox River, from Portage to Green Bay, broken up into 13 segments ranging from 5 to 15 miles long (segment 4 runs through Princeton). The "Heritage Paddle" is described as a "journey of rediscovery" over a part of the route traveled in 1673 by the French explorers Joliet & Marquette, whose traverse down the Fox and the Wisconsin Rivers to the Mississippi River eventually lead to the opening of the Northwest Territory and the great expansion of the United States.

Canoeing, kayaking, fishing, camping, hiking, and cycling opportunities are everywhere. In addition to nearby Mecan and Fox Rivers, Princeton is just minutes away from Green Lake, Lake Puckaway, White Lake, and dozens of other smaller lakes and trout streams. 3 wildlife refuges are within a one hour drive. 150 miles of bike trails wind through the gorgeous countryside.

Worth the drive ten minutes west of Princeton on Highway 23 is the town on Montello. In Montello, and visible from the highway, are 4 beautiful waterfalls that cascade over granite outcroppings. The waterfalls can best be viewed from the Montello Granite Park on Hwy 23. The stone used to create Grant's Tomb was taken this granite park quarry. Montello is also the home to the state's largest tree, a 140' tall cottonwood that towers over downtown.

South of Montello on Hwy F is the boyhood home of naturalist John Muir, the founder of the Sierra Club. His home is now a National Historic Landmark. In 1903, Muir and Teddy Roosevelt took an extended hiking trip through the Yosemite National Park. Shedding the presidential entourage, and with only a handful of National Park employees, the two conservationists spent two nights around a campfire, without tents and with only a pile of army blankets. Waking up covered in snow, TR proclaimed it "the grandest day of my life".

If you're looking for lodging in Princeton, consider Ellison's Gray Lion Inn. Maureen Ellison is a fine hostess and her bed & breakfast features comfortable rooms, great breakfasts, and private baths. Everything in town is within walking distance of the Gray Lion. Call Maureen at (920) 295-4101.

Just outside of Princeton, the Mecan River Outfitters offer several lodging options including their 5 bedroom lodge (with a 35' fieldstone fireplace, bar and restaurant), secluded cabins among the pines, or pitch your tent at one of their primitive campsites. Call (920) 295-3439 or check their website at www.mecanriveroutfitters.com.

THE TAVERN: BUCKHORN LOUNGE

A classic Pabst Blue Ribbon sign hangs outside above the bar's front door. As you enter, you are welcomed by a sign that declares, "Schlitz – go for the gusto", and so we did.

"Do you have Schlitz in bottles?" "No, but we have it on tap. Would you like it in a fancy, tall Schlitz glass?" "Oh yeah"

Critter heads numbering well into double figures adorn the walls. A pool table just inside the front door, darts and video games provide you with fun diversions.

The Buckhorn has a great back deck overlooking the Fox River – you could canoe up to this place! And I'm sure that many people have.

On the back deck are "Hillbilly Wind Chimes": 4 empty beer cans suspended by wires from a wooden sign. Jethro Bodine would agree that this is pretty cool.

The Buckhorn is owned by Karen Rowley, who made sure that we were well fed and watered on her bar's back deck. Karen seems like a genuinely nice person who has the perfect personality to run a tavern. Spending time chatting with Karen makes a Buckhorn visit that much more fun.

Oh yeah, we all liked their food!

Buckhorn Lounge is at 531 West Water Street and their phone is (920) 295-4321.

Sources: Paul Harvey, Prairie State Canoeists, Wisconsin DNR, Wisconsin Paddlers, Friends of the Fox, Princeton Chamber of Commerce, Ken Burns

MILWAUKEE RIVER

MILWAUKEE, WI
TRIP 6.26 MILES & 2 HOURS 52 MINUTES LONG

INTERMEDIATE ABILITY

**LIVERY: LAACKE & JOYS, 1433 N. WATER IN
DOWNTOWN MILWAUKEE 53202, (414) 271-7878,
WWW.LAACKEANDJOYS.COM**

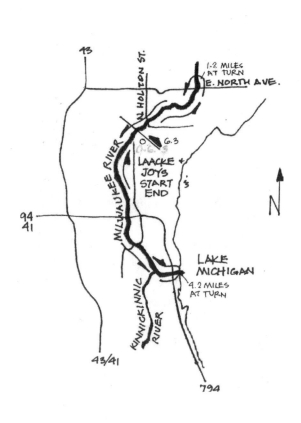

43

N. HOLTON ST.

1.2 MILES
AT TURN
E. NORTH AVE.

MILWAUKEE RIVER

0 6.3

LAACKE +
JOYS
START
END

N

94
41

LAKE
MICHIGAN

4.2 MILES
AT TURN

KINNICKINNIC RIVER

43/41

794

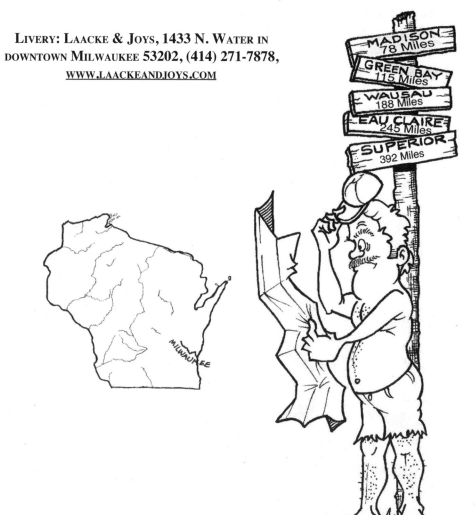

MILWAUKEE

MADISON
78 Miles

GREEN BAY
115 Miles

WAUSAU
188 Miles

EAU CLAIRE
245 Miles

SUPERIOR
392 Miles

THE BACKGROUND: MILWAUKEE RIVER

SOUNDTRACK: JUMP, STOMP & DIVE – WILD
KINGDOM, MESSAGE IN A BOTTLE – POLICE,
LAKE OF FIRE - NIRVANA, DOCK OF THE BAY – OTIS
REDDING, WHAT MADE MILWAUKEE FAMOUS
– JERRY LEE LEWIS

RIVER QUOTE...
ERIC HANSEN: "ARE YOU STEERING OR ARE YOU BEERING?"

The Milwaukee River flows south for 75 miles until it empties into Lake Michigan in the town of Milwaukee. Well before this small stream becomes the wide body of water that meanders through Milwaukee, the main branch of the river absorbs first the west branch, then the east branch, then the north branch – all in Washington County. The trip outlined in this chapter has little in common with the Milwaukee River's rural beginnings.

On the surface (ahem), paddling through a city seems the polar opposite of the setting sought for a canoe or kayak adventure. Once again, a tavern sets us straight (so to speak), as Wolski's Tavern was the inspiration to paddle the Milwaukee. In 2008, while sitting on the riverside deck at Lakefront Brewery, the location for Wolski's 100th birthday celebration, we

watched kayakers float by us on the Milwaukee. We all knew right then and there that this urban paddling adventure was for us. Along the river shorelines, there is a series of floating docks (each 2' above the water line), which make it easy to pull your canoe or kayak over for a tavern or restaurant break. This is an exciting trip that is strongly suggested with its beautiful architecture, drawbridges, and activity along the riverbanks.

The Urban Paddling Team consisted of Neal & David Linkon, Steve Polzin, Pete & Peggy & Kelly Armstrong, Bill & Chris Meeker, Bernadette Kearns, Maggie & Doc.

THE RIVER: PADDLING THE MILWAUKEE

Launch off of the back deck of Laacke & Joys, paddle upstream to North Street, then downstream past L&J to where river empties into Lake Michigan, and then back to L&J.

Departing L&J, turn right off their back deck, and head upstream against the lazy current. The river is 100' wide and wear-your-life vest deep.

.25 mi/10 min: Pleasant Street Bridge, just upstream from L&J.

.5 mi/16 min: Lakefront Brewery on is the western shore (on our left). The Holton Road Bridge is just north (upstream) from the brewery, with its double-stacked upper & lower bridges.

.9 mi/29 min: Humboldt Avenue Bridge.

1.1 mi/35 min: a pedestrian bridge sits upon the ruins of an old dam.

1.2 mi/39 min: paddle against the only rapids of the day, which are just downstream from the North Street Bridge. Rapids are also seen as you look upstream from North Street. Turn around at the North Street

Bridge, and follow the current south to Lake Michigan.

2.3 mi/1 hr 7 min: reach the original launch site at the L&J back deck.

2.4 mi/1 hr 11 min: Cherry Street Bridge, identifiable by its beautiful glass block pieces.

2.5 mi/1 hr 16 min: the Time Warner Cable building on your right is just before the Knapp Street Bridge.

2.6 mi/ 1 hr 20 min: Juneau Avenue Bridge. To the west of the river on Juneau sits the Sydney HiH building. According to crack researcher Bill Meeker, the Sydney was a 1960's hippie gathering place. In 1842, the city's first professional theatre performance took place on this piece of land (an 18-day run of "The Merchant of Venice"). The current edifice was built in 1876. The basement was once home to a very popular Milwaukee night club, "the Unicorn", where Kurt Cobain and Nirvana played on April 8, 1990 in front of 15 people.

Just past Juneau and on the river's left bank is the Harp Irish Pub. Across the river from Harp's is Molly Cool's Seafood Tavern, accessible via the floating dock in front of Molly's. A pedestrian bridge lies just downstream, then "Usinger's Famous Sausage" building is ahead on your right.

2.8 mi/1 hr 22 min: paddle beneath the State Street Bridge. Just beyond the bridge, the "Marcus Center for the Performing Arts" is on your left. The steps on your right lead up from the riverbank to a dome in Pere Marquette Park.

2.9 mi/1 hr 28 min: Kilbourn Avenue Bridge.

3 mi/1 hr 29 min: Wells Street Bridge. On your left, at the corner of Wells & Water St is the Pabst Theater (you're suddenly thirsty). Just past the bridge, on the left is a statue of the Fonz (as Arthur Fonzarelli lives in Milwaukee). Across the river from the Fonz is the Rock Bottom Restaurant & Brewery.

3.1 mi/1 hr 31 min: Just beyond the John Hawks Pub on your left, you've arrived at the Wisconsin Avenue Bridge. Just downstream from the bridge, on your right, is Borders.

3.25 mi/1 hr 34 min: it's the Michigan Street Bridge and the corner of Michigan Street and Riverwalk.

3.35 mi/1 hr 36 min: Clybourn Street Bridge followed quickly by the 794 Bridge. Just beyond 794 and on your left is the Milwaukee Public Market.

3.5 mi/1 hr 40 min: St. Paul Avenue Bridge and a sign for the "Historic Third Ward" is visible beyond the left shore. Downstream from the bridge, and on your left, Buffalo St ends at the river's edge. The north side of the Water Buffalo Restaurant & Bar sits alongside Buffalo Street, and the next door down you've arrived at the Milwaukee Ale House (see "taverns" section), a great break spot.

3.7 mi/1 hr 47 min: the river bends to the left (east) as you float beneath Water Street & the Water Street Bascule Bridge (bascule is a type of drawbridge). Just before this bend, the Menomonee River merges from your right. Downstream from the bridge is the Milwaukee Institute of Art & Design, on your left.

3.9 mi/1 hr 51 min: paddle below Young Street and the Broadway Bascule Bridge.

4.05 mi/1 hr 55 min: Midstream lies the Milwaukee River Bridge, an old abandoned rotating (or "turntable") railroad bridge. Riverfront Pizza is on the left shore.

4.2 mi/2 hours: The Riptide Seafood Bar & Grill is on the left bank as the river bends left (794 is the bridge in the distance), just before it empties into Lake Michigan. This is the turning point for the trip back to L&J.

6.26 miles/2 hours 52 minutes: you're in! Take out at the dock at Laacke & Joys.

THE TOWN: MILWAUKEE

Green Bay Packer local radio station affiliate: WTMJ-AM 620
Milwaukee Brewer local radio station affiliate: WTMJ-AM 620

Before the town of Milwaukee was inhabited by Germans and Pabst Blue Ribbon beer, the Milwaukee River was where the area's main residents, the Potawatomi, paddled their birch bark canoes. The name given the area by an alliance of Native American tribes, led by the Potawatomi, was forever lost by European settler attempts to pronounce it (one of those attempts was "Milwacky"). It was in the early-1800s that "Milwaukee" became the area's popular name. This was a time when the area was thickly covered with a dense and majestic forest that stretched for miles, and when the 3 rivers converging at/near Lake Michigan - the Milwaukee, the Menomonee, & the Kinnickinnic – were so pristine that you could see to the river bottoms (as deep as 18' in the case of the Milwaukee River).

Since Father Jacques Marquette first camped at Milwaukee in 1674, and our nation's subsequent westward migration, development of an area featuring the largest bay and the deepest river (i.e. the Milwaukee River) along Lake Michigan's western shoreline was inevitable. By the 1830s, land speculation had exploded, with ownership of some lots of land changing

hands more than once in a single day and $100 lots selling for $10,000 six months later. Development of the city required demanding physical labor to create streets through the dense wilderness of downtown Milwaukee (no street corners, no street corner bars). Dirt from the many steep bluffs that had to be flattened was used to fill in the marshland found throughout the city. Quite unlike the vibrant Milwaukee of today, 1830s town folk found there was little to do once Lake Michigan was frozen over, temporarily ending traffic flowing into and out of the city's waterfront, except for the non-stop euchre games in session at the local hotels (well, maybe not so much unlike today).

The Father of post-wilderness Milwaukee is Solomon Juneau, a good soul who never let his ambition cloud his decency. Juneau arrived in Milwaukee in 1818 as a fur trader, later becoming a key land developer in the city's earliest stages. His log cabin was the first settler residence in the city, and he built Milwaukee's first Inn and first general store. In 1837, Juneau began printing the "Milwaukee Sentinel", to this day Wisconsin's longest-running business. Juneau was admired and respected by Native American and European settler alike. That reputation led to his becoming Milwaukee's first mayor in 1846. By the time of his passing in 1856, he'd seen the city grow from one non-Native American home (his) to a population of 40,000 (over 600,000 today).

Beer, brats - and brats in beer. No USA city has a higher percentage of citizens with German ancestry then Milwaukee's 48% (in the late-1800s, attendants at Milwaukee's Public Museum were expected to speak English AND German). Not coincidentally, by the time of the Civil War over two dozen breweries operated in the town including the beginnings of the Pabst, Blatz, Schlitz, and Miller Breweries. No city has more bars on its corners, whether in the residential or the commercial sections of town, then Milwaukee. According to a "Men's Fitness" magazine survey, Milwaukee has more bars per capita of any major U.S. city. A drive through town could've saved the money spent on the survey.

Milwaukee's strong Germanic flavor resulted in high tensions during World War I, tensions that did not end when the war did. In October of 1919, 11 months after Armistice Day, downtown Milwaukee's Pabst Theater scheduled a play that was to be done in its original German language. Outraged WWI veterans, with the war against the Hun still fresh in their minds,

placed a cannon next to City Hall, its muzzle focused directly at the theater. The vets' position was if the show goes on, the house comes down. The curtain did not go up.

At different times in its history, Milwaukee has led or been among the world leaders in production of wheat/flour, iron, tanned leather, motorcycles and durable goods/machinery (the city was known as "the machine shop of the world"), but the product that made Milwaukee famous was its beer. Milwaukee's march to become the eventual beer capital of the world began with their first brewery opening in 1841. By the 1860s, the town's beer barons began to sell their product beyond the city limits with great success. And the most successful of Milwaukee's brewers

was the Pabst Brewing Co. Founded by Jacob Best in 1844, the company flourished when Best son-in-law, Captain Frederick Pabst, took over the reins, moving Pabst from a major brand in Milwaukee to the world's leading brewer by the mid-1870s. Could recognition of Pabst as worthy of a blue ribbon at the 1893 World's Fair be far behind?

Milwaukee, where in 1901 William Harley & Arthur Davidson began to work on their first motorcycle, where Golda Meir was born, & where the typewriter was invented.

Milwaukee, where in 1910, for the first time ever in the United States of America, a Socialist was voted in as mayor. Milwaukee's 2nd Socialist mayor, Dan Hoan, was mayor from 1916 to 1940. How do you get elected and re-elected for a quarter of a century? During Hoan's 25-year tenure, Milwaukee regularly won national awards recognizing the town as the healthiest, safest, and best-policed big city in the USA. Rampant corruption among both his Democratic & Republican predecessors was replaced by an honest – and effective - government. The Health Dept. ran outreach programs to eradicate pervasive deadly diseases (the life expectancy in the city when Hoan 1st took office was barely 30 years), he presided over creation of a sewage treatment plant (one still in use today) to end the mixing of drinking water and raw sewage, directed the creation of a world-class park system (including the spectacular Lincoln Memorial Drive along the Lake Michigan shoreline), greatly eased the post-World War I housing shortage by a first-in-the-country municipally sponsored public housing project, and eradicated a cumbersome public debt (a fiscally conservative Socialist!). During the lowest point of the Depression, Hoan's financial acumen allowed for maintenance of city services AND a balanced budget, earning Milwaukee praise from the national press as "an American legend", and a 1936 Time Magazine cover story that suggested Dan Hoan ran "perhaps the best-governed city in the U.S."

Preservationists in Milwaukee have been more successful than their counterparts in most other large cities in saving not only the larger historic buildings (including the Pabst Theater, an outstanding example of restoration over the wrecking ball), but also in reclaiming many older neighborhood residences. There is a unique mosaic of small communities that make up the one Milwaukee, each distinctly different from the next in style, feel, and architectural design. Suburbanites have been drawn back to the natural fireplaces, leaded-glass windows, and hardwood floors found in many of these preserved older homes.

Milwaukee is home to "Summerfest", the world's largest music festival, held each year along the Lake Michigan shoreline. The 1968 inaugural event included an act that had one of its female members strip down to her waist. The lady's subsequent arrest was dismissed by a Summerfest official as "a tempest in a C cup".

Any discussion of Milwaukee should conclude with a reference to what made the town famous, their beer. Should anyone question whether or not the consumption of beer is patriotic, please note that when Prohibition was repealed in 1933, the city of Milwaukee was once again proudly allowed to serve beer in every one of their 1,776 taverns. God bless America!

THE TAVERNS: MILWAUKEE ALE HOUSE & WOLSKI'S TAVERN

Milwaukee Ale House, 233 North Water Street, Milwaukee; (414) 226-BEER

A silo towering high above the Ale House and the river below declares, "Ales What Cures You". Hallelujah sisters & brothers! Nestled within the Historic Third Ward, the Ale House welcomes travelers by sea (well, river) and by land. You could drive here, but it's so much more fun to arrive by canoe or kayak (just over 30 minutes/1 mile downstream from Laacke & Joys). Boat docking is available on a first come first serve basis. Their website tells you the Ale House serves up "fresh music & live beer". Although "6 or more hand crafted beers" are available, you can get a Pabst Blue Ribbon longneck, too – always a sure sign of quality! The Ale House has a full slate of live bands. Both indoor and outdoor seating is offered, with the outdoor riverside tables providing you with a seat right on top of the river. Our group of crack researchers shared a Margherita Pizza, eliciting comments including "Very Good", "Wonderful", "Ex-cel-lant-tay" (Neal, who didn't have a slice, thought it "very light"). Great view, great staff, great food, great drink, great time!

Wolski's Tavern, 1836 N. Pulaski Street, Milwaukee; (414) 276-8130

"Adventure… Danger… Romance" – now THAT'S a bumper sticker! As is "I Closed Wolski's" (a marketing stroke of genius). It's not an easy place to find, but locating it is worth the trouble. Located in Milwaukee's Lower East Side, Wolski's is just east of Humboldt Avenue, north of Brady Street, and a couple hundred feet south of the Milwaukee River. Opened in 1908, Wolski's had one helluva 100 year party in 2008, with the (correctly) anticipated overflow celebration forcing a move

to the Lakefront Brewery. Cozy and comfortable, fair prices, friendly staff and customers. This classic old-time tavern still has its original support beams in place, free popcorn at the ready, and a good time awaitin' you.

Sources: The Making of Milwaukee by John Gurda, www.onmilwaukee.com, Wikipedia, About.com: Milwaukee, Milwaukee Journal Sentinel

NAMEKAGON RIVER

TREGO, WI
TRIP 10 MILES & 3 HOURS LONG

INTERMEDIATE ABILITY

LIVERY: PAPPY'S LEATHERNECKS TAVERN, W8296
US HIGHWAY 77 & COUNTY ROAD F, TREGO WI
54888, (715) 466-2568, WWW.LEATHERNECKSTAVERN.
COM. OWNERS RON AND BONNIE CROSBY.

MADISON 261 Miles
GREEN BAY 262 Miles
WAUSAU 170 Miles
EAU CLAIRE 87 Miles
SUPERIOR 64 Miles

PAPPY'S
77
CO. RD. F
10 CO. RD. F
CO. RD. K
NAMEKAGON RIVER
WHISPERING PINES LANDING
53
CO. RD. F
COUNTY K LANDING
CO. RD. K
N
CO. RD. E
53
NAMEKAGON

THE BACKGROUND: NAMEKAGON RIVER

SOUNDTRACK: MOON DAWG – JOHNNY & THE SHY GUYS, MADISON BLUES – ELMORE JAMES, EGGS – MARTIN MULL, I LOVE THIS BAR – TOBY KEITH, SUMMERTIME – BIG BROTHER & THE HOLDING CO.

RIVER QUOTE...
SIGURD OLSON: "WHEN A MAN IS PART OF HIS CANOE, HE IS PART OF ALL THAT CANOES HAVE EVER KNOWN"

The Namekagon (nam-uh-kah-gun) River headwaters flow out of Namekagon Lake as it meanders for 95 miles through northwestern Wisconsin. For the river's first 60 miles, the Namekagon runs southwest. Once it hits the town of Trego, the river turns northwest for its final 35 miles, ending as it empties into the St. Croix River. Together, the St. Croix & Namekagon Rivers form the 255-mile long St. Croix National Scenic Riverway, one of the first river systems protected by Congress under the 1968 Wild and Scenic Rivers Act.

The stretch of the Namekagon detailed in this chapter is a 10 mile trip, beginning 7 river miles downstream from the town of Trego. The trip ends at the beautiful Whispering Pines Landing. The word "Namekagon" is translated from the Ojibwe and means "place of the Sturgeon". These large fish, found up to 6' in length, can be occasionally spotted in the river immediately downstream from the Trego Dam, where this trip starts. You'll pass by 8 shoreline campsites on the ride, while paddling through multiple riffles and class 1 rapids in the shallow, crystal-clear water. Fish swam by in large numbers and included redhorse suckers, sturgeon, smallmouth bass, and silver channel catfish. We did see eagles and deer, but missed out on seeing a frequent river visitor: word has it that it's not unusual on the hotter summer days to paddle around a bend and see a bear cooling off while sitting in the river.

Canoeing the Namekagon was Kenny Umphrey & Doc. The trip was in June.

THE RIVER: PADDLING THE NAMEKAGON

Launch at the County K Landing, northwest of Trego, and take out at the Whispering Pines Landing. Both access sites have well-maintained restrooms.

As you launch, the Namekagon is 50' wide and 2' deep. Very quickly, the river widens and riffles develop. Two islands are midstream within the first 2/10ths of a mile.

.4 mi/9 min: the river turns extremely shallow, from the left bank across 2/3rds of the river, creating a funnel for class 1 rapids on the deeper right 1/3rd.

.6 mi/12 min: at the end of an S-curve, you see the start of a short (100 yards) class 1 rapids run ahead. You hear these rapids before you see them. Clam shells are on the river floor and along the river banks, "as big as lily pads" says Kenny.

1 mi/20 min: reach the first of 8 DNR-marked campsites on today's float. Stairs lead up to it on the right bank as the river bends left. Just downstream, the river deepens to 3'.

1.5 mi/33 min: just downstream from a creek merging from the left, DNR site #2 is on the left shore. Two deer and an eagle are seen.

1.8 mi/42 min: you're at the upstream end of a long, thickly-treed, island. It will take 8 minutes and .3 of a mile until the downstream tip is reached. The better, faster, water is to the left of the island.

2 mi/48 min: 3rd campsite is accessible at the left shore on a gently-graded slope. In front of the access, the river is 4' deep and makes a great swimming hole.

2.4 mi/58 min: after a long hiatus with no white water, you are in for a treat. It begins with a short class 1 run. Then an island left of midstream, with large rocks ringing its base, heralds the start of a 4 minute class 1 rapids run, through 8 consecutive river bends.

2.8 mi/1 hr 4 min: the 4 minute rapids run comes to an end as the river bends right and where the 4th DNR campsite is found along the right bank. Two 4' diameter rocks, one to the left and one to the right, act as columns leading to the campsite.

3 mi/ 1 hr 7 min: the huge rock on your right, where the river turns to the left, lets you know you're at the 3 mile mark. There is bottom-scraping with riffles.

3.3 mi/1 hr 13 min: on the right shore are 60' high bluffs thick with birch trees.

3.8 mi/1 hr 22 min: Past the stone sandbar on the right as the river bends right, you come upon 3 small islands and one very large one.

4 mi/1 hr 25 min: 50' high bluff along the left bank, with the river 40' across and 2' deep, is followed by a 100' rapids run. After passing a 5' diameter rock on the right shore, more class 1 rapids will follow.

4.4 mi/1 hr 31 min: 4th campsite is seen on the left shore, with stairs leading to it from the river's edge. Not the friendliest slope to pull your boat up on.

4.6 mi/1 hr 34 min: the river bends left as you fly through a rock garden in class 1 rapids.

4.8 mi/1 hr 38 min: real nice class 2 rapids run lasts for only a minute.

5 mi/1 hr 43 min: up log steps on the right bank is campsite #6. Not a particularly good slope to pull your boat up on. The site is fronted by a run of class 1 rapids.

5.9 mi/1 hr 56 min: big steps on the left lead you to campsite #7.

6.2 mi/2 hrs: tall, sandy bluff on the right as the river bends left. Sign at the bottom right tells you, "Sand banks are turtle nesting areas. Please keep off".

6.6 mi/2 hrs 8 min: class 1 run goes for 1/20th of a mile. Stay far left to avoid running aground in the very shallow water. 5' diameter rock lies ahead on the left bend.

6.9 mi/2 hrs 12 min: campsite #8 is on the left bank. Just beyond are riffles on a left turn.

7.1 mi/2 hrs 15 min: a fine break spots lies midstream on the upstream end of an island's sandy beach. Beautiful driftwood pieces are on the island's right.

7.4 mi/2 hrs 21 min: for the next 6 minutes, paddle past several islands, each which may be passed on either side, until the final island. There, the current rockets through on the right, but a log blocks passage on the same side. It's a fun ride if you're willing to stop and drag your boat over the log.

8.8 mi/2 hrs 42 min: A midstream island is passable either left or right.

9 mi/2 hrs 45 min: the first house seen today sits high on the right bank where the river bends left.

10 miles/3 hours: you're in! Whispering Pines Landing is on your right.

THE TOWN: TREGO

Green Bay Packer local radio station affiliate: WRLS-FM 92.3
Milwaukee Brewer local radio station affiliate: WRLS-FM 92.3

The small town of Trego, around 1,000 folks, is located in central Washburn County, in the northwest corner of Wisconsin and 80 miles south of the westernmost corner of Lake Superior. Trego sits on the banks of the Namekagon, right where the river pivots from a southwest to a northwest flow.

In 1882, the area was opened to logging as the first sawmill on the Namekagon River began its cutting. This once quiet stream was soon filled from riverbank to riverbank with logs cut from centuries old pines. When the railroad first came through at the end of the 1880s, the area was known by the railroad men as Superior Junction. The town was created in 1904 under the name of Mills and changed to Trego in 1906. The spring of 1909 saw the Namekagon River's last log drive.

What began as a logging community is now a popular recreational getaway. Besides the wonderful Namekagon River, the Trego area is home to 900 lakes and 200 groomed trails for snowmobiles.

Trego is also where you'll find an excellent river and historical resource, the Namekagon River Visitor Center. The Center is located on Highway 63, 1/2 mile east of Highway 53. Stop in and pick up some of the finest river maps that you'll ever see, including detailed information on riverside camping, wildlife habitat, and find out how the river and the people it has touched have influenced each other for over 1,000 years.

Opening in 2010 in the town of Spooner, 10 minutes south of Trego, was the Wisconsin Canoe Museum, the USA's first wooden canoe museum. The core of the initial museum collection was 29 restored wooden canoes donated by the folks who founded the Wooden Canoe Heritage Association, the Dean Family from Madison. This non-profit venture is a wonderful way to share the beauty of these classic canoes with paddling enthusiasts and with all folks who love history. The museum is located at 312 North Front St. in Spooner.

Camping is available everywhere along the Namekagon. On today's trip, you've passed 8 sites and camping is also available at the Whispering Pines take out. No reservations are taken as these are first come first served. Most campsites feature a metal fire ring, picnic table, and primitive toilet.

Further info on these and other river sites may be found at www.dnr.state.wi.us

THE TAVERN: PAPPY'S LEATHERNECKS TAVERN

At the corner of Hwy 77 and County Road F is a wooden structure. The only sign outside tells you in large letters "Pabst Blue Ribbon" and below in smaller letters "Pappy's Bar". You follow your instinct, and common sense, and go inside.

Once inside, what grabs your attention right away is the helicopter blade suspended from the ceiling behind the bar. The tail rotor blade has printed on it, "U.S. Marine Corp Presidential Helicopter". Bar owner Ron Crosby was a helicopter Sergeant Major Marine escort for President Clinton, and Ron brought this memento of those days to share with Pappy's customers.

As you enter Pappy's, you pass under a sign that says, "Pappy's Bar – my kinda place". And it is. Pappy's employees and customers extended a warm friendliness to out-of-town paddlers. The bar not only sells beer, they also rent canoes and provide lodging at their trailside cabin, a mere 50' stagger behind the bar. There should be a photo of Pappy's in the dictionary under "Nirvana" (1. the state of mind you attain at Pappy's; 2. 90s grunge band). Now, it should be known that, besides bags of chips, pretzels, etc., Pappy's *only* serves pizza. Ok, I guess that'll do ("how fast can you make a 2nd one?").

Pappy's Bar was opened in 1947. When Ron and Bonnie purchased the tavern in 2000, they renamed it "Pappy's Leathernecks Tavern". "Pappy's" was left in the bar's name as a sign of respect for the half-a-century of customers who've enjoyed many a nights here.

"Leathernecks" is the well-known nickname for the toughest fighting organization in the world, the USMC, United States Marine Corps, God bless 'em all! Ron & Bonnie added Leathernecks to the bar's name to honor not only all Marines, but veterans of all the armed services.

The Crosbys have added their own special touch to the bar decorations. Signs behind the bar read, "Terrorist hunting permit – no bag limit – tagging not required" & "Be kind to your bartender – even a toilet can only handle 1 a-hole at a time". The men's room door has a picture of Homer Simpson on it, and Homer is foaming at the mouth, his eyelids half-closed, dreaming of a mug of draft beer over the words, "Got Beer?".

The tavern's trailside cabin has room for 5 and makes a great place to stay after a fun day on the Namekagon River and after a fun night at Pappy's Leathernecks Tavern.

Pappy's is located in Trego at the junction of State Highway 77 and County Road F. Phone (715) 466-2568.

Sources: www.washburncounty.org, www.trego.net, Namekagon River Visitor Center, Bruce Nye, Jack's Canoes, Pappy's employees and customers

SUGAR RIVER

BRODHEAD, WI
TRIP 6.4 MILES & 2 HOURS AND 45 MINUTES LONG

INTERMEDIATE ABILITY

LIVERY: SWEET MINIHAHA CAMPGROUND, N4697 COUNTY ROAD E, BRODHEAD WI 53520, (608) 862-3769, WWW.SWEETMINIHAHA. COM. OWNERS RICK & LISA JOSEPHSON.

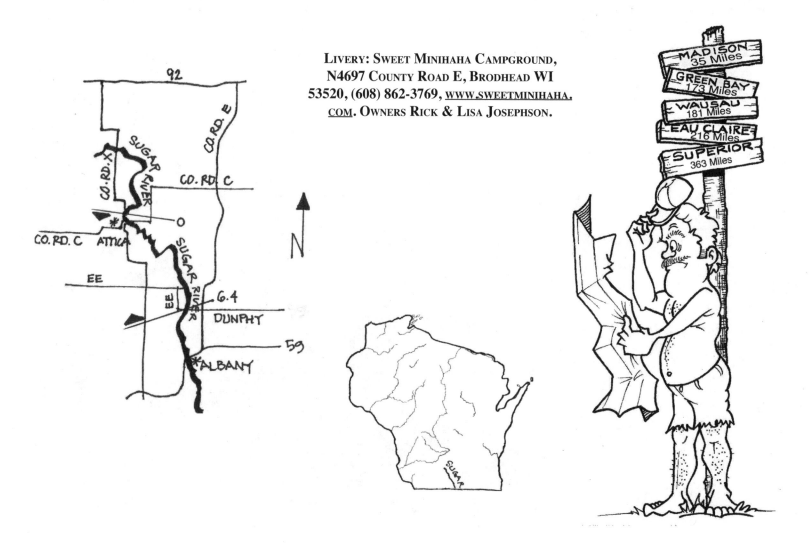

THE BACKGROUND: SUGAR RIVER

SOUNDTRACK: ROTATION – THE SIX SHOOTERS, ME 'N' OPIE (DOWN BY THE DUCK POND) – BR5-49, STUCK IN THE MIDDLE – STEALERS WHEEL (BRIAN & JOHN'S SONG), MOTHER OF PEARL – ROXY MUSIC, BIG JOHN – JIMMY DEAN

RIVER QUOTE:
DAVE: "YOU BOYS *DID* STITCH YOUR NAMES IN THE COLLARS OF YOUR SHIRTS, DIDN'T YOU?"
(AS WE APPROACHED A TREACHEROUS LOOKING LOGJAM)

The Sugar River flows south/southeast for 100 miles. Its headwaters begin about 15 miles SW of Madison, just north of the tiny town of Paoli. From there, the Sugar runs south through Belleville, then turns SE as it meanders through Dayton, Attica, Albany, and then through its southernmost Wisconsin town, Brodhead. From Brodhead, the Sugar River continues SE crossing the Wisconsin – Illinois border and ends 5 miles south of the border where it flows into the Pecatonica River.

The Sugar is not a fast river, averaging a little over 2 miles per hour, but the frequent deadwood & leaning branches encountered adds a keep-you-on-your-toes challenge to your day on the water. Understanding how to steer a boat through the many obstructions is important if you want to enjoy your time on the Sugar River trip outlined below.

Sweet Minihaha Campground offers four different Sugar River trips: (1) a 6-hour float that launches in Attica and ends at their campground, (2) a 3-hour trip from Attica to Albany (this chapter's suggested trip), (3) a 3-hour trip from Albany to the campground and (4) an hour & a-half float that launches just downstream from the Albany dam and ends at the campground.

Sugar River fishing is good with Sheepshead, Northern Pike and Carp. In the merging creeks, Rainbow, Brook and Brown Trout are plentiful.

Floating the Sugar were (local historian) Dave Pryce, his dog Opie, Neal Linkon, Mike Washburn, Jon Hillmer, Brian Barry, John Barry, Maggie & Doc. We paddled in May.

THE RIVER: PADDLING THE SUGAR

Launch at the County Road X Bridge in Attica and take out at the County Road EE Bridge north of Albany.

This stretch of the Sugar River is surrounded by cornfields and dairy farms. There are deep backwaters alongside the river throughout.

You begin just upstream from the County X Road Bridge. Here the river is 50' wide and 4' deep. Over the next half-mile, 4 creeks merge into the Sugar.

1 mi/30 min: 3 logjams have been encountered within the last one-tenth of a mile. Depending on the water level of your trip, one or two portages may be required.

1.2 mi/38 min: a major obstruction blocks the entire river. Stay far left for the least amount of work to get your boat through. 4 minutes downstream is another river-wide fallen tree, but this one provides an opening to shoot through on the far left.

2.2 mi/1 hr 5 min: a very clogged creek merges from the left.

This is not a beginner-friendly stretch of the river: our two canoeing rookies, brothers Big John & Brian, have flipped twice. As in everyday life, a good attitude carries the day and Big John is once again upright and declares, "Woo-hoo! On to the next tree!"

Maggie comments that, "I'm pretty sure that we're not gonna make it home tonight" (the post-Sugar drive to SE Michigan), to which Doc agrees, "It's getting bleaker by the tip".

2.5 mi/1 hr 15 min: a tree-lined island sits midstream and deadwood lies on both sides of the island. The island is passable on both sides in the higher springtime water levels, but you may bottom out to the right in summertime "normal" river levels.

2.9 mi/1 hr 28 min: a little island sits right of midstream. Stay left as the narrower right channel is obstructed.

3 mi/1 hr 33 min: a very large creek merges from the right, about 40' wide at its mouth.

3.7 mi/1 hr 45 min: a cattle fence, which had been running parallel to the river for one-half of a mile, now turns perpendicular to the Sugar. The unseen bellowing cows continue to serenade our little flotilla.

3.8 mi/1 hr 50 min: the river splits around an island. You can paddle either right or left and reconnect 5 minutes downstream at the 4 mile mark of the trip.

4.2 mi/2 hrs: a lagoon lies to the left as the Sugar bends right.

4.4 mi/2 hrs 5 min: as the rivers turns left, on the right shore are farmhouses and a silo. After you round the bend left, you're looking straight ahead at a neighboring farmhouse in the distance.

5 mi/2 hrs 18 min: 30' wide at its mouth, a creek merges left. 3 minutes downstream, arrive at the upstream end of an island.

5.4 mi/2 hrs 26 min: after a creek merges from your left, you come upon a little island that is passable either right or left, but Dave – who knows the river in his sleep – says you'll save 10 minutes if you pass on the left (as paddling to the right takes you into deep backwaters).

5.6 mi/2 hrs 36 min: Allen Creek flows in from the left, labeled by Dave as "an excellent trout stream".

5.9 mi/2 hrs 37 min: arrive at an island as the river bends left.

6.4 mi/2 hrs 45 min: you're in! Float beneath the County Road EE Bridge and exit on the ramp to the right.

THE TOWN: BRODHEAD

Green Bay Packer local radio station affiliate: WCLO-AM 1230/WJVL-FM 99.9
Milwaukee Brewer local radio station affiliate: WCLO-AM 1230

Before the first Europeans arrived in this area, the local residents were the Ho-Chunk Indians, who were also known as the Winnebagos. These Native Americans called the river "Toon-a-Sook-ra", Ho Chunk for "sugar", a reference to the Maple trees along the riverbanks and a reference to the glistening sandstone river bed which resembled sugar.

The French were the first non-natives to discover the Sugar River. These early explorers came looking for riches of gold and silver, but instead found riches of another kind: pearls in clams of the Toon-a-Sook-ra, or Tonasookarah, River. The first Frenchman to discover the river's pearls, a nobleman seeking to replenish his impoverished estate, did not make it back alive to tell the tale, but did write about his find in an animal skin journal that was found along with his bones at the bottom of a bluff near Brodhead.

The first Brodhead area settlers were U.S. citizens who traveled westward from New York State and from New England. When these early settlers arrived, they began calling the river by the white man's name, the Sugar River. By the end of the 1800s, after immigrant settlers began to arrive from Wales, Switzerland, Germany, Norway, Scotland & Ireland, the Sugar River was also known as the River of Pearls due to the clam pearls.

The 1890s "Pearl Rush" brought folks in droves to the Sugar River, as they used hands, feet, rakes, sticks and anything else imaginable to stir the river mud looking for pearls.

Fortunes were made (including a shipment of 60 pearls to England that earned its seller a cash reward of 110,000 pounds) but the Pearl Rush also quickly made extinct the pearl-bearing clams.

"The Half Way Tree": just south of the Brodhead airport, 300 yards off Highway 81, sits an old Burr Oak tree. In the mid-1800s, there was a tribe of Indians who twice a year camped along the banks of the Sugar River on property owned by the Warner family. The camping Native Americans and the Warners were cordial to each other. One day, the tribal chief visited the Warner farm's blacksmith shop to get some guns repaired. The chief pointed to the Burr Oak tree and requested that this tree not be cut down, explaining that the tree marked the halfway point between the Mississippi River and Lake Michigan. Mr. Warner promised that as long as the tree lived it would not be cut, and subsequent owners of the land have kept that promise.

Indians had arrived at the distance between the two places by measuring the number of moons that it took them to walk from Lake Michigan to the Mississippi River. A U.S. Government survey of the land found the halfway mark within 2 and one-half miles from the tree. Since there is some disagreement about the government's method of measuring, perhaps it's the Native Americans who are closer to the exact spot.

Al Ringling, founder of what eventually became known as Ringling Brothers Barnum & Bailey Circus, lived and worked in Brodhead for years before his circus days. Al found work in Brodhead at a wagon & carriage shop in the 1870s.

Al loved a circus, and in his spare time practiced acrobatics and juggling, performing on Brodhead street corners. Word of his abilities soon spread across neighboring communities and beyond. He stretched a tight rope across a downtown Brodhead street, and his tight wire acts became Saturday entertainment for an ever-growing crowd of spectators. Once, Al carried a small stove halfway across the tight wire, stopped to cook a piece of meat, ate his dinner, and then proceeded to the other side. Al Ringling had a well-known desire to have the biggest show on earth. He left Brodhead in 1882 to form his own show, moving to Baraboo WI, where the Ringling Brothers Circus, the "Greatest Show on Earth", was born in 1884. You can read more about the Ringling Bros. in the "Baraboo River" chapter of this book.

Today, Brodhead is a community of 3,200. The downtown has been revitalized, but celebrates its history by carefully restoring many of its older buildings. The Brodhead residents that we met were very friendly and personable. Surrounding the town is a picturesque green and rolling countryside, making for a very scenic drive to the area.

Brodhead is the southern entrance of a bike trail: the Sugar River State Biking & Hiking Trail runs for 23 miles, with its northern end in New Glarus and its southern end in Brodhead. The Trail parallels the Little Sugar River from New Glarus to Albany and then, after the Little Sugar empties into the Sugar, the trail parallels the Sugar River on down to Brodhead.

After a float down the Sugar River, a ride on the bike trail from Brodhead to New Glarus might be a nice idea. New Glarus is a little Swiss village right in the middle of southern Wisconsin. In 1845, the Emigration Society of Glarus, Switzerland, sent representatives to the USA to purchase land for a Swiss settlement. That year, 108 Swiss settled along the Little Sugar River on 1,280 acres of land that these newcomers named New Glarus. Today, America's "Little Switzerland" is a community of just over 2,000. Since 1845, the stream of Swiss immigrants has remained unbroken: the Swiss-German dialect is still spoken, street signs are in both English and Swiss, chalet architecture abounds, and Swiss festivals are held throughout the year. All very nice, but perhaps the best reason for a New Glarus visit has more to do with cows, Spotted Cows to be specific. The town is home to the New Glarus Brewing Co.; makers of, among other beers, Spotted Cow Ale, and a seasonal favorite brew, Totally Naked (leave your loin cloths at home).

The Brewery creates 3,000 gallons of beer per batch and 100,000 barrels a year. The stairway to the fermentation process is the aptly named "Stairway to Heaven". How do I get that goodness in me? Through 5 miles of stainless steel piping. Eventually, 2 waste products result: yeast, which goes on the local farmers' fields, & grain waste, which the farmers feed to their cows, and the cows come 'a runnin!

50 employees… 300 bottles a minute… 60 kegs an hour. New Glarus Brewing Company keeps on rolling… rolling… rolling near a river.

THE TAVERN: FLINAGANS BAR & GRILL

Located in downtown Brodhead, just minutes south of the Sweet Minihaha Campground, is Flinagans Bar & Grill. Flinagans is a great place to grab a bite and a brew after a fun day floating down the Sugar River. Their menu includes burgers, wraps, sandwiches and full dinners. Specials abound during the week, including Taco Thursdays, Fish Fry Fridays, & Bloody Mary Sundays (build your own Bloody Marys while eating Flinagans complimentary wings and cod nuggets). If you happen to be in Flinagans on a Tuesday, & it's the right time of day, you might get one of Barb & Jackie's homemade cookies.

Jackie McCoy & Barb Cole are friendly regulars that now sit on the paying side of the bar (Barb worked here from 1971 to 1985). Along with barkeep Traci Schultz, they shared with us stories of the bar's history. The fine looking rosewood back bar was built in 1906, before this 1912 building was even constructed, and includes an indentation in the wood where a long-ago bar tender used to nervously rub his thumb back and forth (take a look at the back bar's ledge, far left end). A 1920 photo shows that Flinagans was once the M. Hartman Pool Hall. The plaque to the right of the front door states that "This 1912 building is on the National Register of Historic Places, sitting within the Exchange Square Historic District, the Delos Meyers Building, 1912 confectionary & billiard hall".

Today, Marilyn Monroe and Elvis adorn the walls. You can entertain yourself shooting a game of pool, tossing darts, playing video games, or gazing at the collection of over 250 beer cans, including "Billy Beer".

Flinagans Bar & Grill is located at 1034 1st Center Avenue, phone (608) 897-4555.

Sources: special thanks to Dave Pryce, Brodhead Historical Society, www.albany. org, www.brodheadhistory.org, the New Glarus Brewery Co. tour, Wisconsin Official Marker

TOMAHAWK RIVER

MINOCQUA, WI
TRIP 7 MILES & 2 HOURS AND 48 MINUTES LONG

BEGINNER ABILITY

LIVERY: CHEQUAMEGON ADVENTURE COMPANY, 433 EAST
CHICAGO AVENUE, MINOCQUA WI 54548, (715) 356-1618, WWW.
PADDLERAMA.COM. OWNERS ANDREW & SUSAN TEICHMILLER.
THE C.A.C. ALSO PROVIDES SERVICE ON THE TROUT RIVER,
THE MANITOWISH RIVER, THE WISCONSIN RIVER, AND ON
BOTH THE NORTH & SOUTH FORKS OF THE FLAMBEAU.

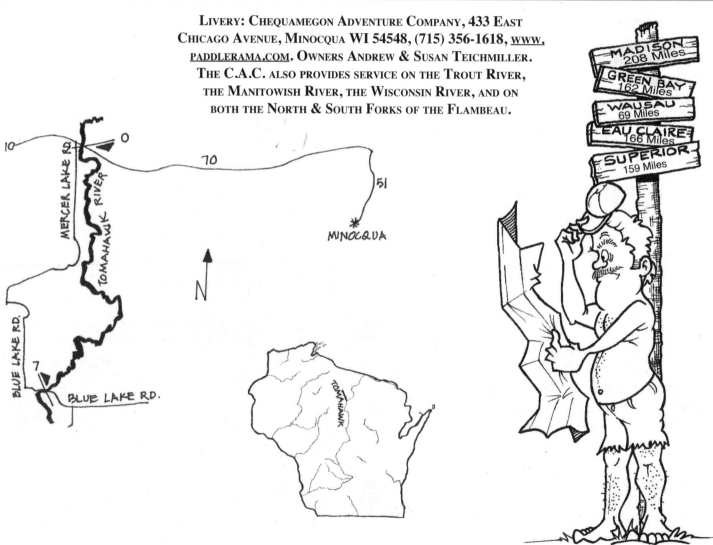

THE BACKGROUND: TOMAHAWK RIVER

SOUNDTRACK: BARSTOOL – DESPERATE OTTOS, APACHE – THE SHADOWS, LONGER BOATS – CAT STEVENS, DON'T BOGART ME – FRATERNITY OF MAN, STORMY WEATHER – BILLIE HOLIDAY

RIVER QUOTES...
KENNY: "TOMMY, YOU CAN'T SAY THAT"
TOMMY: "I CAN. THAT'S WHAT I DO"

The 35-mile long Tomahawk River has its beginnings a few minutes northwest of the town of Minocqua in north central Wisconsin. From its headwaters, the river flows west & parallel to Highway 70 towards Mercer Lake Road. Just before reaching Mercer Lake Road, the river turns south/southwest until it reaches the Willow Flowage. From the Willow Flowage, 22 south flowing miles remain in the Tomahawk's run until it empties into the Wisconsin River.

The section of the Tomahawk outlined in this chapter launches from near the river's headwaters and ends upstream from the Willow Flowage. It is the perfect beginner river, until the somewhat challenging rapids of its final 7 minutes. Long straight-aways predominate, the river width averages 15' to 25', the current flow is laid-back at a little over 2 miles per hour, there are few tight turns, and the river is shallow, usually 6" to 2' deep (Q: what do you do when you tip over? A: you stand up). The flat, grassy riverbanks offer plenty of user-friendly opportunities to pull your boat over for paddling breaks.

The Tomahawk River provided the finest wildlife viewing of any river I've ever been on. We had 4 eagle sightings, 3 groups of deer were spotted, beavers swam by our canoes (beaver dams were everywhere) and there was continuous sightings of geese.

Paddling the Tomahawk was Paul Pienta, Kenny Umphrey, Tommy Holbrook, & Doc. The trip was taken in June.

THE RIVER: PADDLING THE TOMAHAWK

Launch a few feet downstream (south) of the Highway 70 Bridge, 100' east of Mercer Lake Road and 6 miles west of Minocqua. Take out at the Blue Lake Road Bridge, 10 miles southwest of Minocqua.

As the Tomahawk River gentle adventure begins, the river is 20' wide and 2' deep. The opening stretch is a 100 yard long straight-away. The current here is a very slow 1.5 mph.

.5 mi/16 min: a house sits on a high bluff to your right as the river bends left. Just 1/10th of a mile later, the impossible-to-miss large footings of an old bridge are on the left bank.

1 mile/29 min: float beneath a zip line, where the river is 12' wide. The line runs on a descending angle from right shore down to left shore. 5 minutes downstream, the river depth is 4' for a few bends, the deepest that you'll see all day.

1.3 mi/40 min: pilings of an abandoned dock are visible on the right. We float past a very large beaver dam. In 4 minutes, the river shallows and bottom-skimming occurs.

1.9 mi/57 min: float beneath a private road with wooden railings and a gate mid-bridge. You're at the Hamrick LaFrenier Bridge, dedicated to the memory of 9-11.

2.1 mi/1 hr 3 min: a small green home sits beyond the right shore. The river is now 25' wide. Immediately downstream from the green house, a fallen tree blocks all but 5' of the water. Pass on the far left.

2.3 mi/1 hr 9 min: a fine looking home on the right shore is fronted by a 5' x 5' deck.

2.6 mi/1 hr 15 min: encounter back-to-back light rapids runs, each 50' long, as the river pushes you left. A good looking two-level home sits back in the woods 100' on the right, just beyond the rapids. An eagle soars above us with its nest nearby. Our dragonfly escort is keeping us in a mosquito-free zone, God bless 'em.

3.9 mi/1 hr 45 min: a grassy island, 40' long by 20' wide, sits midstream. Downstream 5 minutes there are two bat houses on

the right.

4.4 mi/1 hr 54 min: a long, straight creek merges from your left. Thick reeds are choking the bottom of the Tomahawk.

4.6 mi/1 hr 58 min: back-to-back lagoons are 2 minutes apart.

4.8 mi/2 hrs 2 min: as the river bends sharply left, look over your right shoulder and see a long creek merging right, 12' wide at its mouth.

4.9 mi/2 hrs 6 min: the river makes a big oxbow bending left. At the base of the oxbow lies a straight line cut across (i.e. an oxbow bypass).

5.5 mi/2 hrs 18 min: A deer stand is among the tall pines on the right shore. Look straight ahead and see a house with a stone chimney on a distant bluff, where the river bends left 1/10th of a mile downstream. An eagle sits on a 12' tall dead birch along the right bank.

6.2 mi/2 hrs 34 min: the Tomahawk flows through an oxbow flowing right around an island. It looks like two creeks coming at you as the river bends left.

6.6 mi/2 hrs 41 min: a cabin on the left bank is fronted by an eagle's nest. Here, the river picks up speed as you begin a rapids run through a challenging rock garden. This rapids run takes you through the final 7 minutes of the trip.

7 miles/2 hours 48 minutes: you're in! Float beneath the Blue Lake Road Bridge and take out a few feet downstream from the bridge on the right shore.

THE TOWN: MINOCQUA

Green Bay Packer local radio station affiliate: WCYE-FM 93.7
Milwaukee Brewer local radio station affiliate: WOBT-AM 1240

Midwest Living Magazine rates Minocqua as one of their top 4 family getaways and this quaint little town is deserving of the ranking. Vilas County, where Minocqua resides, is a water-lover's paradise with 73 rivers and streams (including the Tomahawk) and over 1,300 lakes. Field & Stream Magazine says Minocqua is one of the top 20 fishing towns in the USA. In addition to the water fun, you can explore Vilas County's 500,000 acres of forests, its network of trails for hiking, biking & horseback riding, and 600 miles of well-groomed trails for cross-country skiing, snowshoeing and snowmobiling.

Fun fact: the snowmobile was invented in 1924 in the Vilas County town of Sayner by Carl Eliason. Carl called his creation a "motor toboggan". During World War II, the U.S. Army purchased 150 white camouflaged motor toboggans for the defense of Alaska. You can see his original model on display at the Vilas County Historical Museum in Sayner.

Downtown Minocqua and the adjacent residential area are located on what is known as "The Island". This island town lies in the middle of Lake Minocqua. The population of just over 5,000 residents jumps in size several times during the summer. Downtown offers plenty of unique shops, boutiques, and taverns (Otto's Beer & Brat Garden had live music during our Friday afternoon stroll). Stores with names like "Whoops Co." and "Monkey Business" made it almost impossible not to walk in and look around. Even the Minocqua Police Station had a fun look about it, except to the unfortunately incarcerated. Downtown also housed the aptly named "Incite Marketing Co." which, after all, is what marketing is all about.

Minocqua was founded in 1888. Two different stories suggest the origin of the name "Minocqua". One is that it's derived from the Chippewa Indian word "Ninocqua" which means "noon-day rest". The second says the town's name is from the Ojibwa Indians and means "fair maiden". Perhaps we can reach a compromise and propose a noon-day rest with a fair maiden. After all, Running Bear loved Little White Dove with a love big as the sky.

The Ojibwas were the original residents of the island, and remain an important part of Minocqua today. By the late-1800s, the railroad and the logging era changed the area's makeup: in 1891, the town consisted of 15 homes, two hotels, two general stores, a small market, and 29 saloons. It was in the saloons that the lumberjacks could be found when not working among the timber, and until their paychecks disappeared in the shots and the beers.

By the early-1900s, once the stands of pine and hardwood were decimated, the railroads brought folks to Minocqua for a different reason: tourism. The beauty of this area was as hard to resist one hundred years ago as it is today. Among those unable to resist was President Dwight D. Eisenhower, a regular visitor both during and after his time in office.
The fire of 1912 wiped out most of the buildings in the downtown area. The storefronts that you see today are the ones rebuilt after this fire.

It's a short 7-minute walk from the Tomahawk River canoe/kayak livery, Chequamegon Adventure Company, to the Point House Inn Bed & Breakfast. The B&B is found in a picturesque setting on its own peninsula, sitting on a private point surrounded on 3 sides by Minocqua Lake. Point House is a beautiful structure with 5 bedrooms, with lake views from almost every window in the house. Each bedroom has its own bathroom with an extra bathroom on the main floor.

A brick walkway leads from the house to the peninsula's edge, where a fire pit and chairs await you. Not only is the canoe livery nearby, but you're only a 10-minute walk from the B&B to charming downtown Minocqua.

The Point House B&B address is 631 Cedar Street in Minocqua. You can contact owner Elizabeth Kristek at (715) 614-7777 or (715) 358-0212. For more information, go to www.thepointhouseinn.com.

For camping and other lodging options in Minocqua, you can contact their Chamber of Commerce at (715) 356-5266 or check www.minocqua.org.

THE TAVERN: THE THIRSTY WHALE

The Thirsty Whale sits on Lake Minocqua, quite literally, with a great view of the lake from both inside the tavern and from their deck outside. A unique feature of the Thirsty Whale is that the entire pub sits right over the lake.

Over a century of good times has been had in this building, which was erected in 1902. A good deal of that fun began in the 1950s, and ran for over 20 years, with the inauguration of the "Moscow Mule Bucket Club". You could earn a spot in the hallowed club by downing a bucket of Moscow Mule, a drink credited with kicking off the Vodka craze in the U.S. during the 50s. Your emptied bucket was then hung from the ceiling, the sign to all who entered the tavern of your club membership. By the 1970s, the Thirsty Whale's "Moscow Mule Bucket Club" had members in all 50 states and in 7 foreign countries.

Fun Fact: a "Moscow Mule" combines Vodka with Ginger beer and fresh lime juice.

Any bar that provides its patrons with table top shuffleboard is a bar that cares, and this one does. For those looking for other Thirsty Whale diversions, you can choose from shooting a game of pool, throwing darts, playing video games, or grooving to the tunes on the juke box.

Sage Thirsty Whale bartender advice: *Stay vertical and I won't have to throw your drunk ass out!* (they do run a tight ship here, don't they?)

The Thirsty Whale is located along and above Lake Minocqua, at 453 Park Avenue West, phone (715) 356-7108.

Sources: Chequamegon Adventure Company, www.vilaswi.com, Official Wisconsin Travel Guide, Minocqua Visitors Center, www.tn.minocqua.wi.gov, Thirsty Whale dinner menu

WHITE RIVER

Drummond, WI
Trip 6 miles & 2 hours and 25 minutes long

INTERMEDIATE ABILITY

Livery: Bear Country, State Road 63 & Lake Owen Drive, Drummond WI 54832, (715) 739-6645, www.bearcountrysportinggoods.com. Owner Craig & Kathy Manthey.

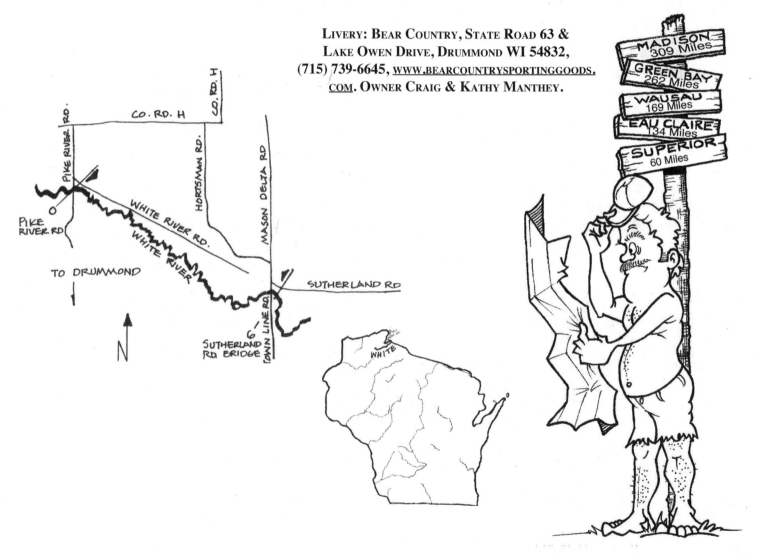

MADISON 309 Miles

GREEN BAY 262 Miles

WAUSAU 169 Miles

EAU CLAIRE 134 Miles

SUPERIOR 60 Miles

CO. RD. H

CO. RD. H

PIKE RIVER RD.

HORTSMAN RD.

MASON DELTA RD.

WHITE RIVER RD.

WHITE RIVER

PIKE RIVER RD.

TO DRUMMOND

SUTHERLAND RD

SUTHERLAND RD BRIDGE

TOWN LINE RD.

N

WHITE

THE BACKGROUND: WHITE RIVER

SOUNDTRACK: THIS WAY OUT – the FURYS, BULLDOZE BLUES – HENRY THOMAS, SHOTGUN – JUNIOR WALKER & the ALL-STARS, LOVESICK BLUES – HANK, STILL RAININ', STILL DREAMIN' – JIMI HENDRIX

RIVER QUOTE...
KENNY: "THIS SECTION OF THE WHITE IS AN ABSOLUTE SPORTSMAN'S PARADISE!"

The White River headwaters rise north of Drummond. From there the river flows for over 50 miles in an east/northeasterly direction, coming to an end as it merges with the Bad River east of Ashland and about a mile south of Lake Superior near the Apostle Islands. The White is well-known among fly fisherman as a great trout stream.

The stretch of the White River outlined in this chapter is flat water absent of rapids. Its current moves quickly through a narrow river bed that's often 15' wide. You experience frequent encounters with tight turns that would like to slingshot you into the tag alders leaning in from the opposite riverbank. This White section is extremely reminiscent of the Upper Peninsula's Fox River, upstream from Seney.

A good deal of paddling experience is required to maneuver through the combination of a narrow stream flowing through tight turns while keeping your canoe or kayak out of the bushes.

Beginning with the 90 minute mark of today's trip, the White River has long stretches of hard-packed sandy floors at 2' depth, providing excellent Frisbee tossing environments. But once the river floor surfaces on to the river banks, it's nothing but muck, so there are very few good riverside locations to pull over for a break at.

This remote stream, running through a lightly-populated part of Wisconsin, provides wonderful solitude along with excellent wildlife viewing as you float downstream.

Canoeing the White during June was Kenny Umphrey & Doc.

THE RIVER: PADDLING THE WHITE

Launch where Cutoff Road meets Pike River Road and take out just past the Sutherland Road Bridge.

Where this White River trip begins, the river is 15' wide and 2' deep.

.7 mi/15 min: pilings are seen along the left river bank. 3 minutes later, a creek merges from the left as the river bends to the right.

.9 mi/20 min: pilings protrude above the water line in 3 parallel rows.

1.2 mi/28 min: a very long and straight creek merges diagonally from the left just before the White turns right. Kenny sez that the "White is a steering, pushing off, and occasional short burst of hard paddling kind of river".

1.8 mi/44 min: paddle beneath the phone lines as the river follows a right hand bend. About 30' in front of us, a deer splashed through the water running from the left to the right river bank. On the left shore, pass by the first home viewed since launching.

2.1 mi/53 min: merging from the right

is a fast-moving small stream, just before the White River bends left. We're irritating a duck that we catch up to every few bends.

2.6 mi/1 hr 5 min: the river narrows to 5' wide, running for several bends with the width fluctuating from 5' to 12' wide.

2.8 mi/1 hr 9 min: a shallow stream enters the river from the right, 4' wide and flowing fast. A blue heron bursts from its hiding place in the left bank bushes and takes flight downstream until it's out of sight.

3 mi/1 hr 16 min: reach the upstream end of an island; the main flow of the river wraps around the island's left, while the water passing on the right is a narrow 4'.

3.2 mi/1 hr 19 min: clear the island's downstream tip; that 4' wide flow passing the island's right reconnects with the main body of the White with terrific speed that indicates flowing right may be a fast and fun run! 3 minutes later, and for the first time today, the river widens beyond 15'. It is now 30' wide and on a long straightaway.

3.6 mi/1 hr 25 min: as the river bends right, there is a 50' long straightaway with a 2' deep, hard-packed sand bottom. Seems to be the perfect Frisbee break area, but hold on…

3.8 mi/1 hr 31 min: the river presents a 150' long straightaway, 40' wide, and is 1 and one-half feet deep – an excellent Frisbee area. The straightaway ends as the river comes to a "T". A large and sprawling creek merges from the right, and is significantly wider than the White River itself. Beyond the "T", the great Frisbee setting continues several bends downstream.

4.3 mi/1 hr 43 min: 3 minutes after the river narrows to 15' wide, an eagle's nest is spotted beyond the left shore. A nest occupant keeps an eye on us and allows us to float nearby for photos.

4.5 mi/1 hr 46 min: a deer stand is on the right shore as the river bends left.

4.6 mi/1 hr 49 min: float beneath phone lines. Here the river is 30' wide and 2' deep.

5.2 mi/2 hrs 10 min: creek merges right and is 4' wide at its mouth.

5.7 mi/2 hrs 19 min: silos viewed beyond the end of a straightaway.

6 miles/2 hours 25 minutes: you're in! Exit to the left just past the Sutherland Road Bridge.

THE TOWN: DRUMMOND

Green Bay Packer local radio station affiliate: WNXR-FM 107.3 & WATW-AM 1400
Milwaukee Brewer local radio station affiliate: WRLS-FM 92.3

The first white men through the Drummond area passed through as a direct result of a 1608 order by the King of France to find a water route to China from New France (a part of what is now Canada). Perhaps finding that route to China was a bit side tracked by explorers who decided instead to stay awhile to soak in the spectacular beauty of the Drummond area. If they filed their report a year or so later, would anyone really notice?

When Kenny called this a sportsman's paradise, he was right on the money. The small town of Drummond has about 600 residents, but that number multiplies several times in the summer months. In fact, folks flock to this town, deep into the Chequamegon-Nicolet National Forest, for fun every season of the year! Beyond the paddling trips down the gorgeous White River, the area has 55 lakes where the boating, camping, swimming, and fishing (trout, northern pike, and walleye) are excellent. In the Fall, the National Forest is spectacular in its golds, reds, and oranges, and the season also brings hunters looking for bear and deer. Winter in the forest provides an escape through its miles of groomed trails for snowmobiles, and its cross-country skiing and snowshoe trails.

But possibly the finest winter time entertainment in Drummond, and maybe in all of Wisconsin, is the Bar Stool Races held each February behind the Black Bear Inn
(see further details below under "The Tavern" section).

45 miles to Drummond's east are the spectacular sights at Copper Falls State Park. You *do* want to take the time to visit the park while you're in the Drummond area, due to a river that you *do not* want to canoe. Cascading and crashing through the park for 8 and one-half miles in a gorge with walls as high as 100' is the Bad River. A 2-mile walking trail takes you both alongside & well above the water for breathtaking views of the river as it takes a roller coaster ride through the steep-walled canyon. The first drop the Bad River takes is a 29 foot plunge at Copper Falls. Further downstream, from a great vista 30' above, you see Tyler Forks merge with the river via a dramatic 30 foot plunge into the canyon over Brownstone Falls. Experiencing Copper Falls State Park will be memorable.

Copper Falls State Park is located 4 miles north of the town of Mellen on State Hwy 169, 25 miles south of Lake Superior, and 26 miles southwest of Ironwood, MI. 55 sites are available at the park's two campgrounds. Call 888-947-2757.

THE TAVERN: BLACK BEAR INN BAR

A few feet away from the front door of the Bear Country livery, you find yourself at a fine place to kick back after a day on the White River. For drinks, dinner, and lodging in Drummond, there's the Black Bear Inn.

The Black Bear Inn opened in 1948. A sign inside the bar reads, "Hunters, Fishermen, & other liars gather here". Waitress Nicki took good care of us. We struck up conversations with several of the bar regulars, who made us feel real welcome.

One of those regulars was a retired Drummond teacher, Del Jerome. We met Del and his wife as they were celebrating their upcoming 50th wedding anniversary. Del has a great knowledge of the rivers and other waterways in Wisconsin. He also knew well the Seney, Michigan, area, so I liked him right off. Del told us that, downstream from the trip that is outlined in this chapter, the White changes quite a bit: approaching the town of Mason there are some short rapids, and great bows in the river where you can see other paddlers floating on a parallel stretch of the river ahead of where you're at. These other paddlers may be only 50' away across the land, but they're 3/4s of a river mile downstream. Besides his river knowledge, it turns out that Del was instrumental in starting up the Drummond Bar Stool Races.

The Bar Stool Races are downhill snow-skiing while riding on bar stools mounted on skis. They have been held each year in Drummond since 2000 on the Saturday of President's Day weekend. The races take place behind the Black Bear Inn Bar. Bear Country livery owner Craig was born in Drummond and moved to Montana where he was exposed to the idea of bar stool races. Craig brought the race idea home with him to stir up some action in Drummond during the town's long winter months. His plan worked as thousands now attend each year. The Discovery Channel sent their crews to the races and their televised segment has contributed to the growing attendance.

There are just a few basic rules to the Bar Stool Races. Among the rules: you may use gravity power only; one bar stool mounted on two skis; all sleds must be inspected by the Race Committee before the race; and all riders must ride the bar stool sitting down, *in drinking position*, butt on top of the stool, and feet not touching the ground. Who knew bar stools could be designed so cool? Check out race videos at www.drummondwi.com and then click on "Bar Stool Racing".

After a fun night socializing in the Black Bear Inn Bar, the adjacent restaurant provides some good chow, and then you retire to the motel section of the Black Bear Inn. Drink, eat, and sleep all in one place. Nice 'n easy.

The Black Bear Inn Bar is located on 15050 Highway 63 & Lake Owen Drive in Drummond, next door to the Bear Country canoe livery, phone (715) 739-6313.

Sources: Craig Manthey, www.drummondwi.com, Wisconsin DNR

WISCONSIN RIVER

TRIP # 1

CONOVER, WI
TRIP 7.5 MILES & 3 HOURS LONG

BEGINNER ABILITY

LIVERY: ROHR'S WILDERNESS TOURS, 5230 RAZORBACK ROAD, CONOVER WI 54519; (715) 547-3639, WWW.RWTCANOE.COM. OWNERS MARCIA & JEFF ROHR.

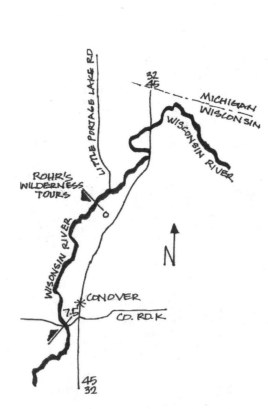

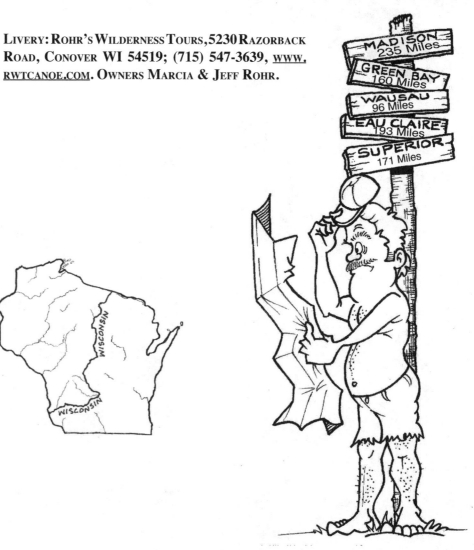

THE BACKGROUND: WISCONSIN RIVER, TRIP 1

Paddling this stretch of the mighty Wisconsin is a surprisingly delightful treat. If you asked most folks how wide the Wisconsin River is, they might answer "a couple of Travis Williams kickoff returns" (i.e. the length of two football fields). Not so in this neck of the woods. Near the town of Conover, the Wisconsin River is a gorgeous, small stream, at times so narrow that each shoulder of a paddler is touching the tag alders leaning in from both riverbanks.

The 430-mile long Wisconsin begins 10 miles north of Rohr's Wilderness Tours livery. The river headwaters flow down from

the high elevation of Lac Vieux Desert Lake, the middle of which is the boundary between Wisconsin and Michigan's Upper Peninsula. From Lac Vieux Desert Lake, the river flows northwest for two miles before turning south/southwest on its way to Conover and eventually to a merger with the Mississippi River at Prairie DuChien, WI. The Wisconsin River remains this narrow stream until it widens after a merger with Eagle River, 33 miles into the 430 mile journey.

This section of the Wisconsin is winding, scenic, secluded, with a laid-back river flow that is beginner and family friendly, and you may see a wide variety of wildlife, from beavers to eagles to bears.

Rohr's offers canoe instruction from beginner to advanced (including a 5-day class 2 whitewater course in the wilderness), and a 40-acre campground along the river and Portage Creek. They will also completely outfit you for your trip, renting or selling everything from canoes, dry bags, and camping equipment to beer. Well, Rohr's won't rent you the beer – you do that.

Paddling the Wisconsin was Tommy Holbrook, Neal Linkon, Jeff Mitchell, & Doc. The trip was taken in July.

THE RIVER: PADDLING THE WISCONSIN, TRIP 1

Launch at the Rohr's Wilderness Tours livery and take out at the County K Road Bridge.

The river is 30' wide as you begin, and the width will vary along the 7.5 mile paddle from 5' to 40'. The sand floor is hard-packed with occasional reeds, stones and, further downstream, rocks on the bottom of the river. At the end of the first straight away is a fine-looking home. This is the only house seen today until the trip's final minutes.

.2 mi/6 min: tag alder bushes lean towards your boat from each river bank. Some bottom-skimming takes place. 10 minutes downstream, the tag alders have majestic pine trees standing behind them.

.8 mi/20 min: great Frisbee area! After the river bends right is a long straight away with an obstacle-free river floor. The river here is 35' wide and 6" deep.

1 mi/25 min: where the river turns left, wind your way through multiple large fallen trees, jutting 2' above the water line.

1.6 mi/42 min: float beneath Rummels Road Bridge where there are two side-by-side bridges, the first vehicular and the second pedestrian.

1.8 mi/47 min: the high sandy bank on the left shore is the

upstream welcome mat to the "Vilas County Forest Wisconsin River Shelter". Climb to the top of the sandy bank and see a campsite, fire pit, shelter with a picnic table, and a Men's & a Women's restroom.

2.2 mi/58 min: as the river bends left, a firmly-implanted large tree, fallen from the right river bank, sits 1' above the water and blocks half of the river.

2.7 mi/1 hr 12 min: a tall, grassy island lies just right of center.

2.9 mi/1 hr 15 min: from the left, Pioneer Creek merges & a large eagle's nest is spotted.

3.1 mi/1 hr 20: the first of many beaver dams seen today. 4 dams on one short straight away leave room to paddle around them. The river turns marshy and tall grass dominates along the banks.

The turns on the Wisconsin River become tighter, requiring a combination of backstrokes and intense, short bursts of paddling to avoid careening into the banks & the tag alders on each river bend.

Ten minutes downstream, we come around a tight bend and see a black bear at the river's left edge getting a drink of water. He quickly disappears into the bush and we're ok with that.

3.8 mi/1 hr 34 min: on the left shore, a channel cuts through the tall grass to a lagoon.

4 mi/1 hr 40 min: beyond the left bank, a nice-looking creek winds through the marshland on its way to a merger with the Wisconsin. Past a beaver dam a big lagoon is downstream and on the right.

4.3 mi/1 hr 48 min: "Mile Marker 15" sign is near the base of a sandy slope on the river's right. This denotes the miles since the beginning of the Wisconsin River headwaters as it flows from the Lac Vieux Desert Lake. In livery co-owner Jeff Rohr's opinion, this is actually mile 16. Pull over here for a nice break location at the top of the sandy slope. The road at the top of the slope is 30' from the river.

Just downstream from Mile Marker 15, a whole series of tiny creeks flow through the marshland, some dead and some active, each 1' to 2' wide feeding the river.

5 mi/2 hrs 6 min: a beaver dam blocks the entire river, forcing a walk-through in the low July water level.

5.6 mi/2 hrs 21 min: Tamarack Creek is the large creek merging from the right. This additional water volume flowing into the

Wisconsin initially widens the river from 15' to 30', deepens the water to 3', and tight turns are replaced by long straight aways.

5.8 mi/2 hrs 26 min: at the upstream tip of an island, a creek merges from the left. From this point on there are frequent sightings of rocks in and along the river. Get ready to dodge rocks up to 4' in diameter.

6 mi/2 hrs 32 min: the river is at its widest today, reaching 40' across. Clam shells lie along the river banks.

6.2 mi/2 hrs 35 min: a tall grassy island sits right of midstream and is christen "wild hair island".

7 mi/2 hrs 52 min: a creek rolls in from the left, 15' wide at its mouth. Just downstream are the remains of a footbridge extending from the left bank. The first home since the initial straight away is seen.

7.5 miles/3 hours: you're in! Exit the river left just before the County K Road Bridge.

THE TOWN: CONOVER

Green Bay Packer local radio station affiliate: WCYE-FM 93.7
Milwaukee Brewer local radio station affiliate: WCYE-FM 93.7

Conover is located in north central Wisconsin, 9 miles south of the Michigan border (16 miles south of Watersmeet, MI) and 9 miles north of Eagle River. The town's eastern edge touches the western border of the Nicolet National Forest. Nicolet contains 660,000 acres of forests, lakes, spring ponds, & rivers, with plenty of opportunities to hike, fish, cross-country ski, hunt, and camp.

Conover itself is home to not only the Wisconsin headwaters, but also 8 large lakes and several smaller lakes and streams. One of those lakes is Lake Pleasant, home of the "Chain Skimmers", a group of amateur water skiers who've been entertaining folks, with various lineups, since 1970. Between Memorial Day and Labor Day, 3 days a week, you can see them entertain with everything from human pyramids to 10-man barefoot lines to trick jumps.

The lure of the area for hunting and fishing led to the town being named Conover. In the late-1800s, a man named Seth Conover would catch a ride on logging trains up to the North and South Twin Lake area for Northwoods getaways. Although no actual train stop existed at the lakes, he had the trains drop him off at his same favorite spot for so many years, the railroad men began calling the stop "Conover's Place". Soon, "Conover" appeared on the official maps of the Chicago and Northwestern Railroads.

The strength of a small Conover girl shines a beacon of hope well beyond the city limits. That small girl is Callie Rohr, the daughter of Marcia & Jeff Rohr. Callie was diagnosed with a brain tumor in 1997. Despite multiple surgeries, radiation, and rehab therapies, Callie passed away in 2000, 5 days before her 10th birthday. Brain tumors are second to leukemia as the #1 medical killer of children under the age of 20.

"The Callie Rohr Memorial Canoe and Kayak Race", held the 2nd weekend in June each year, honors Callie's memory by raising research money to help find a cure for brain tumors. Over $70,000 has been raised in the event's first 6 years, as the funding grows and the cause gains strength, all because of one brave little girl.

A raffle is held during each Callie Memorial event. During one of the raffle drawings, as the winner was being chosen, the sky turned pink – Callie's favorite color.

THE TAVERN: LOG CABIN BAR

Owners Bill and Tori Ellis greet you with a "Welcome to our cabin" sign posted at their bar's entrance. There are several picnic tables that give you the option of outdoor seating, but you want to be inside at the Log Cabin Bar.

The bar has a beautiful pine interior, it's crowded, and a fun feel pervades the tavern. Although swamped with orders shouted from every direction, the waitresses were very pleasant and very good. It's early on a Thursday evening, and the place is packed. A sign behind the bar tells you, "Conover has no town drunk. We all take turns". A large turkey hanging from the ceiling appears to be dead. Also hanging from the ceiling is the replica of a "51 pound 2 ounce muskie, caught by Tom Gelb 11.30.06". Laughter is everywhere. There's a Pabst Blue Ribbon Beer mirror on the wall, always a sure reflection of quality. "Our credit manager is Helen Waite. If you want credit, go to Helen Waite". Next to the credit manager sign is "Tori's Pizza Cave". The large number of folks chowing down on Tori's pie attests to its popularity. The sign above the hallway leading to the restrooms has the letters IITYWTMWYBTHAD. Here one of the waitri showed their patience by explaining to an out-of-towner that the letters stand for…

"If I tell you what this means would you buy the house a drink?" Beautiful.

The Log Cabin Bar is located at 226 Highway 45 in Conover, phone (715) 479-2787.

Sources: Jeff & Marcia Rohr, Wisconsin Historical Society, www.conover.org, Conover Visitor Guide

WISCONSIN RIVER

TRIP # 2
ARENA, WI
TRIP 6.4 MILES & 1 HOUR AND 50 MINUTES LONG

BEGINNER ABILITY

LIVERY: TRADER'S BAR & GRILL AND TACKERS CANOE RENTAL, 6147 HIGHWAY 14, ARENA WI 53503, 800-871-0115 OR (608) 588-7282, WWW.TRADERSBARANDGRILL.BIZ

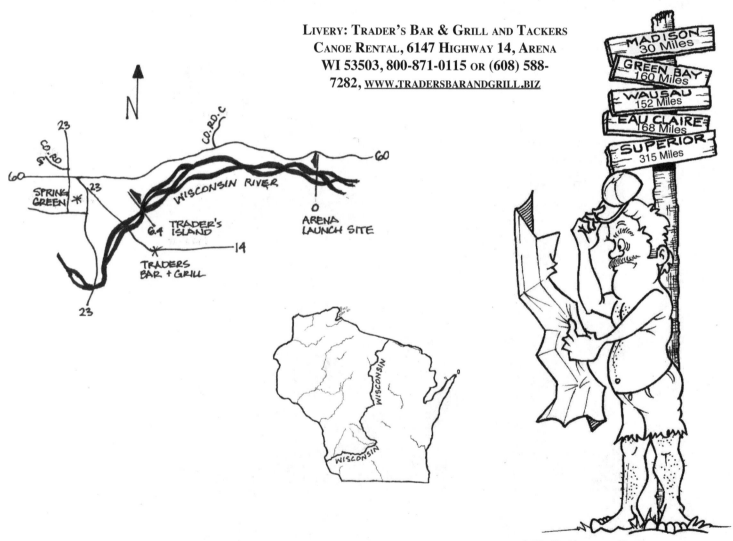

THE BACKGROUND: WISCONSIN RIVER, TRIP 2

SOUNDTRACK: 7-0-7 – THE TORNADOES, SHOTGUN – JUNIOR WALKER (SHOT TOWER TRIBUTE), THE HARDER THEY COME – GRISHAM & GARCIA, CHEESE SHOP – MONTY PYTHON, KASHMIR – LED ZEPPELIN

RIVER QUOTE...
KENNY: "THIS RIVER WOULDA BEEN A *WHOLE* DIFFERENT EXPERIENCE IF WE'D A STAYED RIGHT" (KENNY'S REFERENCE TO THE LAST 2 MILE SIDE CHANNEL EXPLORATION ALONG THE LEFT SHORE)

Along the 430-mile long Wisconsin River, this suggested stretch of the river ends 70 miles upstream from the Wisconsin's merger with the mighty Mississippi River. The peaceful river adventure was enhanced by its ending only 1 mile north of post-float grub & grog at Trader's Bar & Grill, and the fabulous local history including the Spring Green birthplace and Taliesin home of Frank Lloyd Wright, and the ghost town of Helena (see info on FLW and Helena under "The Town" section of this chapter).

The stretch of the Wisconsin outlined in this chapter takes you around dozens of islands, and through environs where turtles numbering in the hundreds entertain with a great plop as they drop off of driftwood pieces into the river in groups of 10s and 20s at a time. The final 2.3 miles of this 6.4 mile float gives you the option of exiting from the football field-wide main body of the Wisconsin River on to a 60' wide side channel along the river's left (south) shore. This side channel is an eagle sanctuary, wind-protected by tall trees along each bank, and is a delightful paddling option.

Floating the Wisconsin in May were Kanoo Kenny Umphrey and Doc.

THE RIVER: PADDLING THE WISCONSIN, TRIP 2

Begin from the Arena Launch site and take out at Trader's Island.

Departing from the Arena Launch site, the Wisconsin is about 300' wide with a depth that ranges from 1' deep near shore to well over your head midstream.

.9 mi/15 min in: should you find yourself seeking relief from a great headwind (always in the realm of possibility when paddling on such a wide expanse of water) an opportunity presents itself just short of 1 mile into the float. Steer your boat to the left of an island that lies near the left shore. The tight channel between the island and the shore, protected by bands of thick forests on both banks, greatly minimizes the headwinds. The channel provides several sandy beach break spots each with fine swimming holes.

1.5 mi/26 min: exiting the sheltering channel, the downstream tip of a mid-river island features a huge sandy beach, a favorite haunt of local geese.

2 mi/34 min: 5 homes are visible on the far right (north) shore hillside, just downstream from an eagle's nest.

2.3 mi/39 min: pass the upstream tip of the first of 3 long, sandy islands. Before passing the downstream end of the 3rd island, a huge eagle's nest is on the left shore.

2.9 mi/47 min: gorgeous midstream island with a large upstream, pullover-friendly, sandy beach. Great wildlife abounds with egrets, geese, ducks, eagles, and turtles-turtles-turtles!

3.4 mi/54 min: 3 "permanent" trailers lie along the left shore.

3.8 mi/1 hour: fine break spot draws your boat in, on the downstream end of a great sandy island across from the left riverbank. It's time to stretch your legs, swim, flip the Frisbee, chow 'n sip.

4.1 mi/1 hr 5 min: stay far left of the large island, marking the beginning of a great 2.1 mile stretch of the river protected by tall trees, completely blocking the wind, on both sides of the water. This side channel adventure features water 60' wide and 6" deep. It feels like you are floating down a wonderful, little, scenic stream – a fascinating diversion from the prodigious main body of the Wisconsin River. It's the Badger State's mini-me to the Atlantic Intracoastal Waterway. One & one-half miles into the channel, 4 eagles circled overhead, and still no sign of the main body of the Wisconsin River. The feel is of being on a completely different river than the one you started on.

5.9 mi/1 hr 43 min: a private residence on the left shore is directly across the channel from the largest sandy beach (it is huge!) paddled by on this trip. It's as if you'd steered your canoe or kayak to the Lake Michigan shoreline. Soon this beach is on both your left and your right.

6 mi/1 hr 45 min: houses and trailers appear along the left bank – the start of the Trader's Island take-out.

6.2 mi/1 hr 48 min: after 2.1 miles, you finally reconnect with the main body of the river. Visible in the distance downstream is a tower and a railroad bridge (the last standing swing bridge on the Wisconsin River).

6.4 mi/1 hr 50 min: you're in! Exit left at Trader's Island.

THE TOWNS: HELENA & SPRING GREEN

Green Bay Packer local radio station affiliate: WIBA-AM 1310 & WIBA-FM 101.5
Milwaukee Brewer local radio station affiliate: WIBA-AM 1310 & WIBA-FM 101.5

Spring Green and the ghost town of Helena are twins separated by the Wisconsin River, located just to the west of Arena and 30 miles west of Madison. Helena, in all 3 of its incarnations, held a place of great importance in the history of and the development of southwestern Wisconsin. Her importance was so great that Helena was once just 2 votes shy of becoming the state capitol - a tale told with pride, and relief, as those 2 votes would've made the area bigger but (in the eyes of local residents who like their home just the way it is) not better. An 1850s bridge built over the Wisconsin River was positioned in such a way that it favored the development of Spring Green over Helena. But before that bridge was built…

In 1828, vast lead deposits were discovered nearby, bringing a population boom to the area and leading to the creation of the first Helena village. The original Helena location was staked out by Henry Dodge, the first governor of territorial Wisconsin (statehood would come in 1848). In 1830, while traveling on the Wisconsin River, Daniel Whitney spotted a sharp bluff that he believed would serve as an ideal location for a shot tower.
Demand for shot (i.e. ammo for guns) was great, driven by the Indian wars, hunters, and fur trappers.

"Shot tower" explanation: lead is melted down, then poured from the top of the shot tower through holes in the side of a large ladle, down the 180' shot tower shaft… falling molten lead assumes a spherical shape and forms "shot"… water at the shaft bottom breaks the shot fall and completes the needed cooling process (did someone stumble upon this OR did some genius mind actually conceptualize this process?).

Creation of the shot tower took 187 days of digging with pickaxes and loosening the more difficult rock with explosives. There was one interruption during the 187 days: the 1832 Black Hawk War. Helena was emptied as the men-folk went off to join militias. When the U.S. Army pursued Black Hawk and his warriors across the Wisconsin River at Helena, they tore down most of Helena's buildings to make rafts. A 1925 historical marker notes that on this "Site of Old Helena on July 28, 1832, troops crossed the Wisconsin River in pursuit of Indians under Black Hawk". These troops were a who's who preview of the Civil War: Lt. Jefferson Davis, Col. Zachary Taylor, Lt. Robert Anderson (in command of Fort Sumter at start of Civil War) and Lt. Albert Sidney Johnston, plus Col. Nathan (son of Daniel) Boone.

After the Black Hawk War, Helena rebuilt a few miles northeast to its 2nd location. The shot tower was completed & the town prospered in the mid-1830s to the mid-1850s due to income & job creation from the large exports of lead shot. Helena's success was considered to be a major factor in the settlement of southwestern Wisconsin: shipping lead shot created a major road and rail line from Helena east (Milwaukee was a prime destination), and returning traffic on the road & rail brought settlers who populated the territory beyond Helena and throughout the southwest Wisconsin territory all the way to the Mississippi River.

Two factors keyed the end of Helena: (1) the Panic of 1857 and (2) the placement of a railroad bridge over the Wisconsin River which favored Spring Green at the expense of Helena. The town was moved one final time to be along this new rail line, but worsening economic times in 1860 resulted in the sale of the town's assets and the abandonment of Helena. The shot tower, which played such a major role in the expansion of Wisconsin, ceased production in 1861 and soon fell into decay.

The property that the shot tower sits on was purchased in 1889 for $60 by a Unitarian minister, the Reverend Jenkin Lloyd Jones. Realizing the tower's historical significance and appreciating the beauty of the location, Rev. Jones created a retreat called the Tower Hill Pleasure Co. The retreat became a nationally known educational and recreational destination, complete with 25 cottages, a restaurant, and buildings where visiting lecturers, books, and music could be enjoyed. Upon Jones death in 1918, his widow donated the site to the state, and the Tower Hill State Park was christened in 1922. A visitor today to Tower Hill State Park can view a reproduction of the shot tower at its original site, and camp out while enjoying the park's many nature and hiking trails. For further information, click on http://www.stateparks.com/tower_hill.html

In 1911, the Reverend Jones nephew began building his architectural studio on a hill near the shot tower bluff. Jones' nephew was Frank Lloyd Wright and the studio was Taliesin, a piece of information that leads us into the story of Helena's sister town, Spring Green. Spring Green was founded amidst the Panic of 1857. The town's name is attributed to the first female settler in the area, a Mrs. Turner Williams, who asked that the surveyors name the land "Spring Green" because "to the north of her house, in the hallows facing south, the green came so much earlier in the spring than in the surrounding country". Spring Green's first settlers were hardy Welsh (including the parents & grandparents of Frank Lloyd Wright), German, Norwegian and English folk. These immigrant's main industries were cheese, dairy, & lumbering. While agriculture remains an important part of today's Spring Green economy, the area has become widely known for its art and its architecture, drawing visitors from far and wide to visit Taliesin, the American Players Theatre (one of the most popular outdoor classical theaters in the country), The House on the Rock, and a variety of artist studios and galleries. The most famous of these, by far, is Taliesin.

Frank Lloyd Wright once said, "Early in life, I had to choose between honest arrogance and hypocritical humility. I chose the former and have seen no reason to change." Born 1867 in nearby Richland Center, Frank spent childhood summers on a family farm just outside of Spring Green. After graduating from the University of Wisconsin, and then a period of creating architectural magic in Oak Park (Chicago) Illinois, Frank returned to the peacefulness of Spring Green to build his 600-acre Taliesin home. This was Wright's principal residence for the rest of his days. Taliesin is a Welsh (his family lineage) term meaning "shining brow" or "radiant brow" (the home is on the "brow" of a hill), and its design reflects how greatly Frank was influenced by what he saw on his travels to Europe and Japan. Located on the estate are 5 structures designed by Frank, and he used Taliesin as a laboratory to experiment with ideas that eventually were used on future Wright designs. Taliesin became a National Historic Landmark in 1976.

Wright's creations melded the structure with the site, bringing the outdoors indoors (his creation "Falling Waters" in southern Pennsylvania is a brilliant example of this). Among Frank's pioneering ideas are earthquake-proof structures (his Imperial Hotel in Tokyo was one of the few buildings left standing during the 1923 quake), pre-fabricated homes, gravity heat, and indirect lighting.

There is an architectural driving tour of the Spring Green area that will take you to 14 structures designed by Wright or former associates and apprentices including homes, banks, churches, cottages, farms, motels, and the Spring Green Chamber of Commerce.

THE TAVERN: TRADER'S BAR AND GRILL

Trader's is located at 6147 Highway 14 in Arena WI, just to the east of the Wisconsin River and just minutes from the Old Helena shot tower. Trader's address may say Arena but their heart says Helena. The tavern is ground zero for the history and living memory of Helena, and co-owner Terry Askevold is ground zero's heartbeat. An afternoon spent in Trader's (a fine idea in and of itself) listening to Terry is a fascinating walk through Helena's history. His passion for the Helena story is reflected in the naming of his (and co-owner Abby Schultze) tavern as "Trader's", recognizing that Helena was once an important fur trading post.

A fine-lookin' riverside tavern that also rents canoes and kayaks is very hard to pass up, and we suggest that you don't. Owners Terry and Abby, and their burly friend Bill, make strangers immediately feel welcomed. Entering Trader's between the totem poles, you're walking into knotty-pine comfortable. Besides the interesting conversation, entertainment comes in the form of pool tables, a juke box, darts, video games, TVs and Trader's wall signs (right next to the Pabst wall clock)…
1. "Returned checks: $50 and a slap."
2. "Beer, not just for breakfast anymore."
3. (below drawing of a baseball bat) "Attitude adjustment while you wait."
4. "This is not Burger King – you don't get it your way, you take it my way, or you don't get the damn thing."

Leinenkugel beer on tap, poured for you with love through 8" tall canoe-shaped tappers. Lord, I do believe that I'm home.

Sources: Terry Askevold, Centennial Spring Green the First Hundred Years, Forgotten Villages: Helena by Beulah Folkedahl, Tower Hill State Park historical markers, www.absoluteastronomy.com, Wikipedia, www. springgreen.com, Wisconsin Official Markers

WISCONSIN RIVER

TRIP # 3: INTO THE MISSISSIPPI RIVER
PRAIRIE DU CHIEN, WI
TRIP 9 MILES & 3 HOURS

VETERAN ABILITY

LIVERY: CAPTAIN'S COVE CANOE AND KAYAK RENTAL, 13389 US HWY 18, PRAIRIE DU CHIEN WI 53821; (608) 994-2860, WWW.CAPTAINSCOVECANOEING.COM. OWNERS HARRY AND KIT KLOTZ.

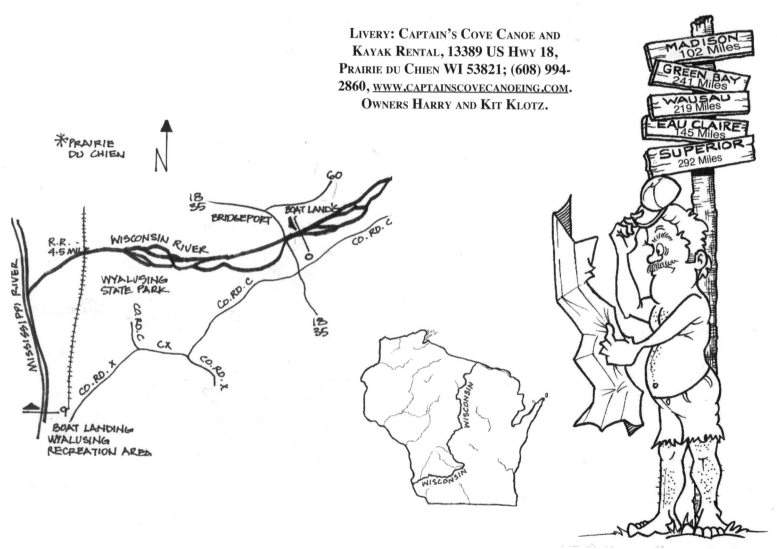

THE BACKGROUND: WISCONSIN RIVER, TRIP 3

SOUNDTRACK: TIC TOC – THE CONTINENTALS, MISSISSIPPI MUD – HANK WILLIAMS III, OLD MAN RIVER – PAUL ROBESON, BIG IRON – MARTY ROBBINS (RANDY & DAVID VOGT TRIBUTE), SONG OF THE VOLGA BOATMAN – SMOTHERS BROTHERS, THE END - THE DOORS

RIVER QUOTE...
MISTER P ON THE 35-40 MPH HEADWINDS: "IT'S LIKE WE'RE FLOATING *INTO* CLASS 2 RAPIDS"

In the language of the Algonquian, "wees-konsan" means "the gathering of the waters". For the original residents of the state and the early European arrivals, the Wisconsin River was *the* major water highway for travel, trade and adventure. Beginning at its Lac Vieux Desert Lake headwaters (north of Conover WI & south of Watersmeet MI), the Wisconsin River meanders in a south and southwest direction for 430 miles. It finally comes to an end as it empties into the Mississippi River near Prairie du Chien. Due to its almost 50 hydroelectric plants and reservoirs, the Wisconsin River is called the "hardest working river in America".

The Wisconsin River trip outlined in this chapter takes the longest river in the state to its end at the merger with the Mississippi, as you float the final 6 miles of the Wisconsin and then 3 miles of the Mississippi. Just north of the merger of these two great rivers, Prairie du Chien WI and McGregor, Iowa face each other across the Mississippi River.

Strong winds may be encountered on the wide open spaces of the lower Wisconsin River. Due to the 35 to 40 mph headwinds that met us, the usually quiet river had whitecaps as far as the eye could see. Although the current was with us, rolling waves were coming at us and occasionally splashing into our canoes.

Due to the strong headwinds that can kick up on such wide bodies of water, and because of the large amount of Mississippi big boat traffic, this trip receives a "veteran ability required" rating. The entire Wisconsin-Mississippi River experience is fabulous and you know immediately it's one that you'll always treasure.

The Wisconsin-Mississippi paddlers were Paul "Mister P" Pienta, Toni LaPorte, Neal Linkon, Chris Weaks, Kenny Umphrey, Maggie & Doc. This trip was taken in May.

THE RIVER: PADDLING THE WISCONSIN, TRIP 3

Begin the journey from the Bridgeport Boat Launch, located 5 miles southeast of Prairie du Chien on Highway 18/35. This is the last canoe landing on the Wisconsin River. The trip ends on the Mississippi River at thc Wyalusing Boat Landing.

Upon launching, you immediately arrive at the upstream end of Weniger Island. You may pass on either the wider right (north) or the more narrow (80' wide) left channel. The narrow left channel offers some protection from strong winds. The water here is over-your-paddle deep.

1.5 mi/30 min: the two channels reunite as you reach the end of one & a half mile long Weniger Island. A small grassy island lies midstream just beyond.

2.5 mi/50 min: the wide sandy beach on the right shore is an enticing spot to pull over for a break. The river here is about a quarter-mile wide.

3 mi/1 hr: two great sandy beaches are side-by-side on the right bank. Across the river and beyond the left shore is the northern edge of Wyalusing State Park.

3.5 mi/1 hr 10 min: on the left is a quiet creek offering shelter from the winds. The creek, although full of obstructions during our journey, does rejoin the main body of the river over a mile downstream, just before the railroad bridge.

4.5 mi/1 hr 30 min: within clear view of the downstream railroad bridge is a very long & very wide beach on the left bank. Eagles circle overhead during a beach break. *While on the beach, Chris gave us his four river tips: (1) wear old baseball spikes on the river, cutting slits to let the water out, (2) using a* <u>horizontal</u> *dry bag allows you to find your gear easier, (3) a campfire chair with a footrest is a must and (4) always bring a baseball cap for river dipping and then back on the head for an energy burst.*

4.7 mi/1 hr 33 min: downstream from the great left shore beach, you paddle beneath the railroad bridge. Starlings flock under the bridge by the hundreds.

200 yards beyond the bridge, a creek flows to the left. You may take this as a bypass to both the Wyalusing Canoe Trail and the Mississippi River. The creek is well-sheltered from any strong winds that may be on the Wisconsin.

5.5 mi/1 hr 50 min: get your first glimpse of the high bluffs across the Mississippi River, including two homes built near the top of a bluff. Mississippi River barges are visible. We're not on the Kickapoo River anymore, Toto.

6 mi/2 hrs: the 430-mile long Wisconsin River comes to an end as it empties into the 2,552-mile long Mississippi River. You'll turn left and flow south on to the Mississippi.

At the merger, there's a tiny spit of land on the left. Pull your kayaks and canoes over, and take in a little bit of history. Marquette and Joliet stood here in 1673 as they sought a river highway that would take them from the Upper Great Lakes to the Gulf of Mexico. From Upper Lake Michigan, they paddled through Green Bay down the Fox River to the Wisconsin River and, shortly after arriving at this spot, they knew that they had found the river highway that they had sought.

Buoys are midstream as you enter the Mississippi. Here the river is relatively narrow and, surprisingly, not as wide as the Wisconsin River was. It is suggested that you paddle within 50' to 70' of the left shore to minimize the impact of waves created by passing large boats.

Within 5 minutes of merging on to the Mississippi, the Wyalusing Canoe Trail begins on your left. This trail provides fun exploration opportunities on quiet flat water.

8 mi/2 hrs 40 min: reach the upstream end of a large grassy island that is fronted by a miniature red-roofed lighthouse. The island is to the left of midstream. Paddle to the island's left. It takes 6 minutes to reach the island's downstream tip.

9 miles/3 hours: you're in! Take out on the left shore at the Wyalusing Boat Landing beach in the town of Wyalusing. The boat landing has restroom facilities. From here, you can look upstream (to your right while facing the Mississippi) and actually see the point where the Wisconsin River entered the Mississippi River.

THE TOWN: PRAIRIE DU CHIEN

Green Bay Packer local radio station affiliate: WQPC-FM 94.3
Milwaukee Brewer local radio station affiliate: WQPC-FM 94.3

Prairie du Chien is an area rich with history. It is the oldest European settlement on the Upper Mississippi River. The area was visited by the French explorers Marquette & Joliet in 1673 making them the first Europeans to see the Upper Mississippi. French influence is found in the town's name, "la Prairie des Chiens", French for "Prairie of the Dog", a reference to the Fox Native Americans who lived on the prairie east of the river.

Once discovered by the French, the town became a popular place to conduct the fur trade, as it had been for centuries

before among Native Americans. Its position at the western end of a waterway connecting the Great Lakes and Green Bay with the Mississippi made it a natural gathering spot. A trading fort was soon built by the French, and a common sight from the late-1600s to the early-1800s was to see Indians and French on the prairie trading pelts for guns and other manufactured goods. The importance of the trade could be seen in establishing la Prairie des Chiens as neutral territory where warring tribes laid down their arms to attend the trading rendezvous.

The French often married Native American women and these European settlers lived in harmony with the area's original residents. This harmony dissolved when the young United States eventually moved into the area, regulating the trading to a degree not seen before and pushing the Native Americans off of their ancestral lands to unfamiliar areas to the west. Since the French bought the land that their homes were on from the Native Americans, and since the original Indian ownership was no longer recognized by the USA, many French lost their homes and property in the early 1800s.

The fur trading era is brought back to life each year at Prairie du Chien's "Prairie Villa Rendezvous". The Rendezvous re-enacts the fur traders lives and is the largest such re-enactment in the Midwest. Held annually on Father's Day weekend, an estimated 25,000 attendees make their way from all over the country to Prairie du Chien. Rows of tents and teepees are set up, the cooking fires are going, furs are displayed, folks learn about the medicines of the day, basket

weaving and bead working seminars are held, and the period costumes look great (love those hats!). The smell of Indian fry bread and Buffalo Burgers fills the air. Rendezvous games (hopefully before the grog is consumed) feature the axe toss, bow and arrow accuracy, and shooting competition with gunpowder-packed long rifles. To top it all off, there's great song & dance brought back to life from days gone by.

While canoeing and kayaking the Wisconsin to the Mississippi, an excellent site for camping is at the Wyalusing State Park. The park is at the southeast corner where the Wisconsin and the Mississippi Rivers meet. From a bluff 500' above, the park offers a fabulous view of the confluence of these two great rivers. At Wyalusing you can view Indian burial mounds, waterfalls, beautiful rock outcroppings, and historical markers. You can float down a canoe trail, fish, boat, picnic, bike or hike 23 trail miles, visit the interpretive center and just plain enjoy nature. Wyalusing's 2,628 acres includes 2 campgrounds with 109 sites, a lodge that holds 108, and a group tent campground for 130. Call (608) 996-2261 and check out www.wyalusing. org.

Across the Mississippi from Wyalusing is another great camping spot at Pikes Peak State Park in McGregor, Iowa. Pikes Peak claims to have the highest bluff on the Mississippi River at a little over 500'. As does Wyalusing, Pikes Peak provides a spectacular view of the merging of the Wisconsin and the Mississippi Rivers. 77 campsites are offered along with plenty of hiking trails and picnic areas. Call (563) 873-2341.

THE TAVERN: DEW DROP INN

Chick-a-boom, chick-a-boom, don't ya jes' love it? I guess that Daddy Dewdrop knew what he was talking about, 'cause we love this place.

Any ad that suggests that you "visit the Dew Drop Inn for strong drinks, delicious Bloody Mary's, cheap beer, tasty burgers, good conversation, and beautiful sunsets" shows that the ad's author knows how to pull the folks in off the streets. Plus, the bar's location is a good one, only two miles from the Wyalusing State Park entrance. Along with all of those excellent reasons to spend time in the Dew Drop are the fun personalities of owner Adam Hubanks and his friend, bar help, and co-conspirator Bruce.

Adam offered Bruce money for his time helping out at the tavern. Bruce said, "No, just free beer." Adam said that this turned out to be an expensive proposition for him.

When asked if he thought he'd be working awhile, Bruce replied, "I ain't working now!"

The "I closed Wolski's" bumper sticker behind the bar caught our attention. Adam said that the only reason he remembered he'd been to Wolski's that blurry evening was "when I pulled the bumper sticker out of my backside."

Adam owns a real comfortable tavern, one that you could easily spend a few hours too many in. Walking in, one of the first things that greeted us was a round table perfectly suited for the afternoon of euchre that broke out. It turns out that winter-time Sunday night euchre tournaments are a regular Dew Drop Inn happening. Summertime is Saturday night live bands and DJs.

Adam bought the bar from his Dad, Mike, in 2008. When it was Mike's bar, old-timers would let themselves in before the bar was opened, drink beer, play euchre, and help themselves to cheese and crackers. By the time Dad arrived to open up the tavern, they were gone and the till was always right.

California bikers stopped by once when they couldn't find a place to camp. Adam let them stay for free, setting up their tents on the hill next to the Dew Drop. Adam sized the guys up to be good men, and overnight he left the bar door open so that the bikers could access the restrooms. They kiddingly asked if they could help themselves to his bar. Adam replied, "Guys, I have guns inside and they're all loaded." Twelve guys lifted their shirts, each revealing a gun, smiled and said, "Us, too!"

The Dew Drop Inn is located at 12761 County Road X in Bagley, ph (608) 996-2243.

Sources: Prairie du Chien Chamber of Commerce, Michael Douglass, Rogeta Halvorson, Mary Antoine "The Forts on the Mound", Wisconsin Historical Markers, Currents Through History

WISCONSIN CANOE LIVERIES

BARABOO RIVER

Baraboo @ Riverside Rentals 608-356-6045, 608-434-2468
103 Ash St., Baraboo, WI 53913
Beyond Boundaries 608-464-7433
Old Tald's Feedmill
113 Center St., Wonewoc, WI 53968
www.goingfarbeyond.com

BARK RIVER

Rock River Canoe Rental 920-728-0420
Jefferson, WI 53549
www.rockrivercanoerental.com

BEAR RIVER

Hawk's Nest Canoe Outfitters 800-688-7471 (all year)
263 US Hwy. 51, Manitowish Waters, WI 54545
(Phone summer only: 715-543-8585)
www.hawksnestcanoe.com

BLACK RIVER

Black River Canoe Rental 715-284-8136
N5399 St. Hwy 54, Black River Falls, WI 54615
Black River Express Canoe Rental 608-488-7017
301 S Washington St., Melrose, WI 54642
Hatfield Sports Shop 715-333-5009 (hauling by appointment)
N451 Hwy. J, Hatfield, WI 54754
www.hatfieldsportsshop.com
Lost Falls Campground LLC 715-284-7133, 1-800-329-3911
N2974 Sunnyvale Rd., Black River Falls, WI 54615
www.lostfalls.com
Riverview Inn 608-488-5191
N608 North Bend Dr., Melrose, WI 54642
www.riverviewinn.biz
Silent Glide Canoe and Kayak Shop 715-748-0148
W6821 Wester Ave., Medford WI 54451
www.silentglidecanoeandkayakshop.com

BOIS BRULE RIVER

Brule River Canoe Rental 715-372-4983
13869 E. US Hwy. 2, Brule, WI 54820
www.brulerivercanoerental.com

BRULE RIVER

Northwoods Wilderness Outfitters 906-774-9009, 1-800-530-8859
N4088 Pine Mountain Rd., Iron Mountain, MI 49801
www.northwoodsoutfitters.com

CHIPPEWA RIVER

Chippewa River Canoe Rental 715-462-9402
7596W Pinepoint Rd., Hayward, WI 54843

Corral Bar & Riverside Grill Canoe & Kayak Rental (715) 672-8874
318 West Main, Durand, WI 54736
www.corralbarandriversidegrill.com

Flambeau Adventures, LLC 715-532-7733
N7788 Flambeau Rd., Ladysmith, WI 54848
www.flambeauadventures.com

Flater's Trailer Park & Campground 715-595-6244
N270 Co. Rd. E, Holcombe, WI 54745
www.flatersresort.net

Loopy's Log Cabin 715-723-5667
10691 Co. Hwy. X, Chippewa Falls, WI 54729
www.723loop.com

Riverside Bike & Skate 715-835-0088
937 Water St., Eau Claire, WI 54703
www.riversidebikeskate.com

Silent Glide Canoe and Kayak Shop 715-748-0148
W6821 Wester Ave., Medford WI 54451
www.silentglidecanoeandkayakshop.com

Wannigan Resort 715-266-5141
N5909 Dam Rd., Winter, WI 54896

CRAWFISH RIVER

Rock River Canoe Rental 920-728-0420
Jefferson, WI 53549
www.rockrivercanoerental.com

EAU CLAIRE RIVER

Riverside Junction 715-456-2434
S5550 St. Hwy. 27, Augusta, WI 54722
www.riversidejunction.com
Riverside Bike & Skate 715-835-0088
937 Water St., Eau Claire, WI 54703
www.riversidebikeskate.com

FLAMBEAU RIVER-NORTH FORK

Big Bear Lodge 715-332-5510
W1614 Co. Hwy. W, Winter, WI 54896
www.bigbearlodgeww.com
Flambeau Adventures, LLC 715-532-7733
N7788 Flambeau Rd., Ladysmith, WI 54848
www.flambeauadventures.com
Flater's Trailer Park & Campground 715-595-6244
N270 Co. Rd. E, Holcombe, WI 54745
www.flatersresort.net
Hatfield Sports Shop 715-333-5009 (hauling by appointment)
N451 Hwy. J, Hatfield, WI 54754
 www.hatfieldsportsshop.com
Hawk's Nest Canoe Outfitters 800-688-7471 (all year)
263 US Hwy. 51, Manitowish Waters, WI 54545
(Phone summer only: 715-543-8585)
www.hawksnestcanoe.com
Nine Mile Tavern Canoe Rentals 715-762-3174
W10590 St. Rd. 70, Park Falls, WI 54552
www.parkfalls.com/ninemile
Oxbo Resort 715-762-4786
6275N Oxbo Drive, Park Falls, WI 54552
www.oxboresort.com

FLAMBEAU RIVER-SOUTH FORK

Big Bear Lodge 715-332-5510
W1614 Co. Hwy. W, Winter, WI 54896
www.bigbearlodgeww.com
Chequamegon Adventure Co. 715-356-1618
8576 Hwy. 51 N, Minocqua, WI 54548
www.paddlerama.com
Flambeau Adventures, LLC 715-532-7733

N7788 Flambeau Rd., Ladysmith, WI 54848

www.flambeauadventures.com

Flambeau Sports Outfitters 715-339-2012

N11151 Co. Rd. F, Phillips, WI 54555

www.flambeausports.com

Flater's Trailer Park & Campground 715-595-6244

N270 Co. Rd. E, Holcombe, WI 54745

www.flatersresort.net

FOX RIVER

Aqua Guides and Outfitters, Inc . 262-618-4868, 262-339-2664

N65 W6899 Cleveland St., Cedarburg, WI 53012

www.aquaguideandoutfitter.com

Fox River Landing 262-662-5690

31421 Bridge Dr., Waterford, WI 53185

Mecan River Outfitters 920-295-3439

W720 St. Rd. 23, Princeton, WI 54968

GALENA RIVER

Fever River Outfitters 815-776-9425 (hauling by appointment)

525 S. Main St., Galena, IL 61036

www.feverriveroutfitters.com

GRANT RIVER

Grant River Canoe & Kayak Rental 608-794-2342 (appointment only)

7961 Co. Rd. U, Grant, WI 53802

www.grantrivercanoerental.weebly.com

ILLINOIS FOX RIVER

Tip A Canoe LLC 262-342-1012

139 W. Chestnut St., Burlington, WI 53105

www.tipacanoellc.com

JUMP RIVER

Flambeau Adventures, LLC 715-532-7733

N7788 Flambeau Rd., Ladysmith, WI 54848

www.flambeauadventures.com

Silent Glide Canoe and Kayak Shop 715-748-0148

W6821 Wester Ave., Medford WI 54451

www.silentglidecanoeandkayakshop.com

KICKAPOO RIVER

    Crooked River Resort 608-629-5624
    Hwy. 61 S., Readstown, WI 54652
    www.crookedriverresort.com
    Drifty's Canoe Rental 608-337-4288
    Hwy. 33, Ontario, WI 54651
    www.driftyscanoerental.net
    Kickapoo Yacht Club 608-625-4395
    S2463 Rockton Loop, Rockton, WI 54639
    www.kickapooyachtclub.com
    Mr. Ducks Canoe Rental 608-337-4711
    100 Main St., Ontario WI, 54651.
    www.mrduckscanoerental.com
    Titanic Canoe Rental 1-877-438-7865, 608-337-4551
    St. Hwy. 131N & Main, Ontario, WI 54651
    www.titaniccanoerental.com
    Wisconsin River Outings 866-41 canoe, 608-375-5300
    715 Wisconsin Ave., Boscobel, WI 53805
    7554 US. Hwy. 12, Sauk City, WI 53583
    www.86641canoe.com

KINNICKINNIC RIVER

    Kinni Creek Lodge & Outfitters (877) 504-9705, 715-425-7378
    545 N Main St., River Falls, WI 54022
    www.kinnicreek.com

LA CROSSE RIVER

    Elli Stone Canoe & Ḳayak Rental, LLC 608-343-5696, 608-487-5114
    N5370 Co. Rd. J, Bangor, WI 54614
    www.ellistonecanoerental.com

LEMONWEIR RIVER

    Country Cruisin' Canoes & Kayaks 608-548-4280
    Mauston, WI 53948
    www.castlerockpetenwell.com

LITTLE WOLF RIVER

    Wolf River Trips & Campground 920-982-2458
    E8041 Co. Trk. X, New London, WI 54961
    www.wolfrivertrips.com

MANITOWISH RIVER

Chequamegon Adventure Co. 715-356-1618
8576 Hwy. 51 N, Minocqua, WI 54548
www.paddlerama.com
Coontail Sports 715-385-3399
5454 Park St., Boulder Junction, WI 54512
www.coontailsports.com
Hawk's Nest Canoe Outfitters 800-688-7471 (all year)
263 US Hwy 51, Manitowish Waters, WI 54545
(entire length--phone summer only: 715-543-8585)
Ruggers Landing Resort 715-476-2530
5643 Hwy. 51N, Mercer, WI 54547
Schauss Woodwork 715-385-2434
10305 Main St., Boulder Junction, WI 54512

MECAN RIVER

Lake of the Woods Campground 920-787-3601
N 9070 14th Ave., Wautoma, WI 54982
www.lakeofthewoodswi.com
Mecan River Outfitters 920-295-3439
W720 St. Rd. 23, Princeton, WI 54968

MENOMINEE RIVER

Kosir's Rapid Rafts 715-757-3431
W14073 Co. Rd. C, Silver Cliff, WI 54104
www.kosirs.com
Northwoods Wilderness Outfitters 906-774-9009, 1-800-530-8859
N4088 Pine Mountain Rd., Iron Mountain, MI 49801
www.northwoodsoutfitters.com

MILWAUKEE RIVER

Aqua Guides and Outfitters, Inc . 262-618-4868, 262-339-2664
N65 W6899 Cleveland St., Cedarburg, WI 53012
www.aquaguideandoutfitter.com
Laacke & Joys 414-271-7878
1433N Water St., Milwaukee, WI 53202
www.laackeandjoys.com

MINK RIVER

Bay Shore Outdoor Store 920-854-7598
2457 S. Bay Shore Drive, Sister Bay, WI 54234
www.kayakdoorcounty.com

MONDEAUX RIVER

Silent Glide Canoe and Kayak Shop 715-748-0148
W6821 Wester Ave., Medford WI 54451
www.silentglidecanoeandkayakshop.com

MONTREAL RIVER

Whitecap Kayak 906-364-7336
930 E. Cloverland Dr., Ironwood, MI 49938
www.whitecapkayak.com

NAMEKAGON RIVER

Bear Country Sporting Goods 715-739-6645 or 888-847-7869
P.O. Box 130, Drummond, WI 54832
www.bearcountrysportinggoods.com

Camp Namekagon RV Park 715-766-2277
W2108 Larson Rd., Springbrook, WI 54875
www.campnamekagon.com

Hayward KOA Campground 715-634-2331
11544 N. U.S. Hwy. 63, Hayward, WI 54843
www.haywardcamping.com

Jack's Canoe Rental 715-635-3300
N7550 Canfield Dr., Trego, WI 54888
www.jackscanoerental.com

Log Cabin Resort 715-635-2959
N7470 Log Cabin Drive, Trego, WI 54888
www.logcabin-resort.com

Pappy's Canoe Rental 715-466-2568
W8296 Hwy. 77, Trego, WI 54888
www.pappyscanoes.com

Pardun's Canoe Rental & Shuttle Service 715-656-7881
7595 Main St., Hwy. 77, Danbury, WI 54830
www.pardunscanoerental.com

Wild River Bar 715-634-2631
10167 St. Rd. 27, Hayward, WI 54843

Wild River Outfitters 715-463-2254
15177 St. Rd. 70, Grantsburg, WI 54840
www.wildriverpaddling.com

PAINT RIVER
    Northwoods Wilderness Outfitters 906-774-9009, 1-800-530-8859
    N4088 Pine Mountain Rd., Iron Mountain, MI 49801
    www.northwoodsoutfitters.com

PESHTIGO RIVER
    Kosir's Rapid Rafts 715-757-3431
    W14073 Co. Rd. C, Silver Cliff, WI 54104
    www.kosirs.com
    Mt. Jed's Camping & Canoe 715-757-2406
    W13364 Co. Rd. C, Silver Cliff, WI 54104
    Peshtigo River Campground 715-854-2986
    W7948 Airport Rd., Crivitz, WI 54114
    www.peshtigorivercampground.com

PIKE RIVER
    Mt. Jed's Camping & Canoe 715-757-2406
    W13364 Co. Rd. C, Silver Cliff, WI 54104

PINE RIVER
    Northwoods Wilderness Outfitters 906-774-9009, 1-800-530-8859
    N4088 Pine Mountain Rd., Iron Mountain, MI 49801
    www.northwoodsoutfitters.com
    U. P. Wide Adventure Guide 906-430-0547
    W6508 Epoufette Bay Rd., Naubinway, MI 49762
    www.upwideadventureguide.com

RED CEDAR RIVER
    Corral Bar & Riverside Grill Canoe & Kayak Rental (715) 672-8874
    318 West Main, Durand, WI 54736
    www.corralbarandriversidegrill.com

RIB RIVER
    Silent Glide Canoe and Kayak Shop 715-748-0148
    W6821 Wester Ave., Medford WI 54451
    www.silentglidecanoeandkayakshop.com

ROCK RIVER
    Blue Heron Landing 920-485-4663
    Hwy. 33 at the Bridge, Horicon, WI 53032
    www.horiconmarsh.com

SHEBOYGAN RIVER
    Aqua Guides and Outfitters, Inc . 262-618-4868, 262-339-2664
    N65 W6899 Cleveland St., Cedarburg, WI 53012
    www.aquaguideandoutfitter.com

SILVER CREEK
    Silent Glide Canoe and Kayak Shop 715-748-0148
    W6821 Wester Ave., Medford WI 54451
    www.silentglidecanoeandkayakshop.com

ST. CROIX RIVER
    Eric's Canoe & Kayak Rentals 651-270-1561
    Hwy 35 & 8, St. Croix Falls, WI 54024
    www.ericscanoerental.com
    Jack's Canoe Rental 715-635-3300
    N7550 Canfield Dr., Trego, WI 54888
    www.jackscanoerental.com
    Log Cabin Resort 715-635-2959
    N7470 Log Cabin Drive, Trego, WI 54888
    www.logcabin-resort.com
    Pardun's Canoe Rental & Shuttle Service 715-656-7881
    7595 Main St., Hwy. 77, Danbury, WI 54830
    www.pardunscanoerental.com
    Wild River Outfitters 715-463-2254
    15177 St. Rd. 70, Grantsburg, WI 54840
    www.wildriverpaddling.com

SUGAR RIVER
    Crazy Horse Campground 608-897-2207, 800-897-6375
    N3201 Crazy Horse Lane, Brodhead, WI 53520
    www.crazyhorsewi.com
    Minnihaha Campground 608-862-3769
    N4697 Co. Rd. E, Brodhead, WI 53520
    www.sweetminihaha.com
    S & B Tubing, Canoeing & Kayaking 608-862-3933
    100E Main St., Albany, WI 53502

TOMAHAWK RIVER
    Chequamegon Adventure Co. 715-356-1618
    8576 Hwy. 51 N, Minocqua, WI 54548
    www.paddlerama.com

TREMPEALEAU RIVER

Safehouse Bar & Grill & River Rat Outfitters 608-539-4001, 608-539-2882
N20281 Co. Rd. J, Dodge, WI 54625
www.safehouseriverratoutfitters.com

TROUT RIVER

Chequamegon Adventure Co. 715-356-1618
8576 Hwy. 51 N, Minocqua, WI 54548
www.paddlerama.com
Coontail Sports 715-385-3399
5454 Park St., Boulder Junction, WI 54512
www.coontailsports.com
Hawk's Nest Canoe Outfitters 800-688-7471 (all year)
263 US Hwy. 51, Manitowish Waters, WI 54545
(Phone summer only: 715-543-8585)
www.hawksnestcanoe.com
Schauss Woodwork 715-385-2434
10305 Main St., Boulder Junction, WI 54512

TURTLE RIVER

Hawk's Nest Canoe Outfitters 800-688-7471 (all year)
263 US Hwy. 51, Manitowish Waters, WI 54545
(Phone summer only: 715-543-8585)
www.hawksnestcanoe.com
Ruggers Landing Resort 715-476-2530
5643 Hwy. 51N, Mercer, WI 54547

WHITE RIVER

Bear Country Sporting Goods 715-739-6645 or 888-847-7869
P.O. Box 130, Drummond, WI 54832
www.bearcountrysportinggoods.com
Unlimited Trophy Outfitters 715-413-0336 (hauling by appointment)
www.unlimitedtrophyoutfitters.com

WISCONSIN RIVER

Bender's Bluffview Canoe 608-544-2906
E10032 Huerth Rd., Sauk City, WI 53583
www.canoelady.com
Blackhawk River Runs 608-643-6724
10032 Co. Rd. Y, Mazomanie, WI 53560
Captain's Cove Motel & Canoe & Kayak Rental 608-994-2860
13389 US Hwy. 18 at Co. Rd. C, Prairie du Chien, WI 53821

www.captainscovecanoeing.com

Chequamegon Adventure Co. 715-356-1618

8576 Hwy. 51 N, Minocqua, WI 54548

www.paddlerama.com

Country Cruisin' Canoes & Kayaks 608-548-4280

Mauston, WI 53948

www.castlerockpetenwell.com

Eagle Cave Resort 608-537-2988

16320 Cavern Lane, Blue River, WI 53518

www.eaglecave.net

Eric's Canoe & Kayak Rentals 651-270-1561

Hwy 35 & 8, St. Croix Falls, WI 54024

www.ericscanoerental.com

Grouse River Canoe Adventures 715-310-9460

2804 Co. Rd. II, Steven's Point, WI 54481

www.grouserivercanoeadventures.com

Hawk's Nest Canoe Outfitters 800-688-7471 (all year)

6141 Hwy. 70 West, Eagle River, WI 54521

(from headwaters to Rainbow Flowage-summer only: 715-479-7944)

Corner of Hwy. D & St. Hwy. 47 South, Lake Tomahawk, WI 54539

(from Rainbow Flowage to Rhinelander--summer only: 715-277-3144)

www.hawksnestcanoe.com

Point Bluff Resort 608-253-6181

3199 Hwy. Z, Wisconsin Dells, WI 53965

www.pointbluff.com

River's Edge 608-254-7707

20 Rivers Edge Rd., Wisconsin Dells, WI 53965

www.riversedgeresort.com

River View Hills Canoe Rental 608-739-3472

24678 St. Hwy. 60, Muscoda, WI 53573

Rohr's Wilderness Tours 715-547-3639

5230 Razorback Rd., Conover, WI 54519

www.rwtcanoe.com

Silent Glide Canoe and Kayak Shop 715-748-0148

W6821 Wester Ave., Medford WI 54451

www.silentglidecanoeandkayakshop.com

Trader's Bar and Canoe Rental 1-800-871-0115, 608-588-7282

6147 St. Hwy. 14, Arena, WI 53503

www.tradersbarandgrill.biz

Waz Inn 608-583-2086

234 S. Oak St., Lone Rock, WI 53556

Wisconsin Canoe Co. 608-432-5058

(Lower Wisconsin)

Intersection of Hwy. 23 & 14, Spring Green, WI 53588

www.thebestcanoecompanyever.com

Wisconsin River Outfitters 715-277-2555

Lake Tomahawk, 54539

www.wisconsinriveroutfitters.com

Wisconsin River Outings 866-41 canoe, 608-375-5300

715 Wisconsin Ave., Boscobel, WI 53805

7554 US. Hwy. 12, Sauk City, WI 53583

www.86641canoe.com

Wisconsin's Riverside Resort, Inc. 608-588-2826

S13220 Shifflet Rd., Spring Green, WI 53588

www.wiriverside.com

WOLF RIVER

Bear Paw Outdoors 715-882-3502

N3494 Hwy. 55, White Lake, WI 54491

www.bearpawoutdoors.com

YAHARA RIVER

Kegonsa Cove 608-838-6494

2466 Co. Rd. AB, McFarland, WI 53558

www.kegonsacove.com

YELLOW RIVER

Country Cruisin' Canoes & Kayaks 608-548-4280

Mauston, WI 53948

www.castlerockpetenwell.com

Silent Glide Canoe and Kayak Shop 715-748-0148

W6821 Wester Ave., Medford WI 54451

www.silentglidecanoeandkayakshop.com

PADDLING & CAMPING CHECKLIST

bug spray	sun block
plastic drop cloths (rain)	trash bags
dry (waterproof) bags	ziplocks
water	food
forks/plates	music
nose strips (for our loud friends)	ear plugs (see nose strips)
reynolds wrap (grub leftover)	small pillow
large ziplocks	first aid kit
sleeping bag	tent
knife	clothesline rope
pots/pans/large spoon	grill/grate
fire starter/matches	blankets
2 sets of keys	river shoes/dry shoes
Thermarest/air mattress	river & dry clothes
bungee cords	cooler, ice, water
frisbees	campsite chairs
rain poncho	flashlights
towel	soap, toothpaste/brush
toilet paper	euchre decks
can opener	camera
baseball cap	$$$ & wallet
handtowel/paper plates	sunglasses